# EYES OF THE NIGHT

*Witchcraft among a*
*Senegalese People*

# EYES OF THE NIGHT

*Witchcraft among a*
*Senegalese People*

WILLIAM S. SIMMONS    *University of California, Berkeley*

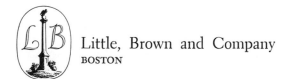

Little, Brown and Company
BOSTON

*To my Mother*

# Acknowledgments

This book is based upon fieldwork among the Badyaranké of the village of Tonghia in Senegal. To the people of Tonghia, who so graciously looked after me during those many months, I owe my greatest debt.

Witchcraft was not an easy subject to explore, and I would have learned very little had it not been for my principal research assistant, Kamara Abdullae Emile. Since witchcraft was a dark subject to the Badyaranké, a number of details and names in the case histories have been changed.

Professor Robert Gessain and his wife Monique, of the Centre de Recherches Anthropologiques in the Musée de l'Homme in Paris, invited me to live in their home during my preparations for the trip to Senegal. The Gessains advised me about the kinds of problems encountered in the back country of Senegal, and through them, I first learned of, and became interested in, the Badyaranké people. To them I owe many pleasant memories, both in Paris and in Africa.

Much of the information in Chapter 2 appeared in an article entitled "Social Organization among the Badyaranké of Tonghia, Sénégal," which was published in the *Cahiers du Centre de Recherches Anthropologiques* in 1967. Professor Gessain, who is editor of this journal, has given permission for the inclusion of this material. Some of the data in Chapter 3 appeared in "The Supernatural World of the Badyaranké of Tonghia (Sénégal)," an article published in the *Journal de la Société des Africanistes*, Tome 37, fasc. 1, 1967, pp. 41–72. Germaine Dieterlen, who also contributed to my preparations before entering the field and who is Secretary-General of the Société des Africanistes, has given permission to include portions of the article.

The results of my fieldwork were incorporated in my doctoral dissertation, "Seers and Witches among the Badyaranké of Senegal"; this was written under the direction of Professor Douglas Oliver, and was accepted by him for the Department of Anthropology at Harvard University in 1967. Many thanks go to Professors William W. Howells and J. O. Brew for helping to procure financial assistance during the final years of graduate study. The Senegalese fieldwork was made possible by two grants, a Frederick Sheldon travelling fellowship and a Charles H. Smith bequest scholarship, both of which were awarded by Harvard University. Thanks also go to my brother, Robert M. Simmons, who patiently helped with the final proofreading of the book.

# Contents

# EYES OF THE NIGHT

*Witchcraft among a*
*Senegalese People*

CHAPTER ONE

*Owls*
*and Other*
*Night People*

THE BEGINNING AND THE END

During my first evening at the village of Tonghia, I watched the Badyaranké women dance and sing in an adjoining compound. A woman drummed upon a gourd bowl which floated upside down on the surface of a tub of water, while one and sometimes two women entered the circle and danced barefooted. Small boys tended a fire of cornstalks and grass, and did dances among themselves, and a few men laughed as they watched from the shadows. The women were singing, so I was told, about how much suffering there is in the world.

My second day was spent giving away aspirin and dropping medicine into inflamed eyes. I ate with the chief, sitting on the dirt floor of his thatch-roof house, and learned to scoop rice and a little sauce into my fingers, molding this mixture into a ball by using one hand. At midday we sat on the shaded side of his

1

FIGURE 1   THE APPROXIMATE LOCATION OF THE VILLAGE
OF TONGHIA

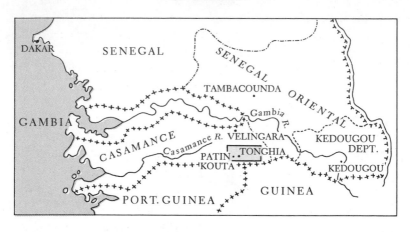

house and the chief taught me to count up to ten in the Badyaranké language. He indicated the numbers with his fingers, and
each time we reached ten he would laugh. An elder brought us a
gourd filled with palm wine which the chief and I drank from a
tin cup. The taste was unfamiliar to me, but sweet and pleasant.

That evening, after the village onlookers had left my doorway
and I had finally fallen asleep, a gun discharged close by, jolting
me awake. Men with swords and muskets gathered in the compound, talked for a while, then laughed among themselves, and
went back to their houses. I later learned that the chief's son, my
next door neighbor, had been bothered by a large owl hooting
from the top of his roof. He had fired at the bird "with eyes and
ears like a man" because it was thought to be a Badyaranké who
had come to collect a human life. Despite the owl's appearance
coinciding with my arrival, the villagers did not believe this owl
to have been me, for although anyone, including an anthropologist, might become an owl, such persons only harm friends,
relatives, and neighbors among their own people.

Large owls did not appear in the village again until thirteen
months later, on the night before my departure. By this time, I
knew the horror that this bird evoked, and I could understand
enough of the language to follow what people said. The chief

2

came out of his house wrapped in a blanket, stood in the middle of our compound in the moonlight, and addressed the birds as they hooted from a tree. He said angrily, "If someone dies here I will call Lawalli.[1] It has been a long time since *comidyidyi* has been here. You want to start something here again. I know about you. I am the only one who dares to get up and face you." The chief's son then turned a flashlight on the tree and fired his muzzle-loading musket, causing an enormous explosion and a fountain of sparks. Still the birds remained. My assistant, who had patiently been helping me to understand such matters as these during the preceding nine months, first called to me for help. Then he pleaded with two French hunters — from whom I hitched a ride out of the bush — who were spending the night in the village. He asked them to shoot the owls out of the tree, and they obliged by firing several shotgun blasts in the direction of the sounds. Something white fluttered away in the darkness and then all was quiet. The next morning I left the compound for a world where the sounds and movements of the night mean nothing. I explained to the puzzled hunters that the cries they heard were from the throats of restless souls which had flown to the village to announce that a life had come due.

## THE BACKGROUND

The preceding incidents are especially vivid memories since they took place during my first fieldwork as a student of social anthropology, when I lived in Senegal, West Africa, with the Badyaranké from October 1964 to January 1966. I first heard of this little tribe from Monique and Robert Gessain of the Musée de l'Homme in Paris, who had worked for a number of years among the neighboring Coniagui and Bassari tribes. The Gessains said that many Badyaranké remained pagan despite centuries of familiarity with the Islamic Sudanese empires, that their social system was poorly understood, that their household groupings were large and perhaps symbolically arranged, and that the men were often blacksmiths, a craft replete with magical pretensions. Thus the

[1] A marabout, Lawalli is described on page 102.

Badyaranké seemed to hold much promise for the student of custom.

My research objectives were two-edged. I hoped to become familiar with the mystical forces that animate the Badyaranké's tiny domain, learning how these are recognized, cajoled, avoided, or otherwise communicated with. To phrase this first objective somewhat differently, I sought the Badyaranké's unique interpretation of such universal events as sickness, death, and prosperity. The second and primary goal was to explore the relationship between these mystical conceptions and the exigencies of social living.

Although I was delighted to be introduced to an unfamiliar cast of sprites, genies, and witches, my principal interest was to determine how such beings illuminate people's behavior. The Badyaranké tell fascinating stories about a long-legged sprite (*ufann*), who haunts damp, lonesome glades in the bush and guards nature's resources. Such folkloric details were a necessary prelude to an understanding of what services ufann provides, which persons avail themselves of his services, and how such people are regarded by their relatives and neighbors. These questions could only be approached through background knowledge of the individuals involved and by direct observation of the vicissitudes in their behavior. I sought, in the real world of human ambition, envy, and suffering, the ingredients that contributed to Badyaranké suspicion that one or another mysterious being is meddling with men's destinies. Eventually I learned that to these people mystical power was not possessed solely by invisible, crepuscular spirits, but was exercised by, or attributed to, certain of my neighbors and even my friends in the village. With this realization I sought to clarify how such individual power was distributed, with which people and situations it was associated, and what, if any, results could be attributed to it.

INTRODUCTION TO TONGHIA

To reach the Badyaranké of Senegal, I proceeded from Dakar on the coast to the bush country of the Upper Casamance by rail and by truck. At the town of Tambacounda, I met a young Badyaranké, a monitor in a Catholic mission school, who agreed to accompany me for the remaining three weeks of his vacation and to work as my interpreter and assistant. Our trek brought us first to the Badyaranké village of Sare Oura, where my interpreter's parents were living. We were welcomed with the effusive and endless Badyaranké salutations: "Hello, good evening. Good evening, hello. How is your mother? How is your father? How is your brother? Hello, how are the children?" We were brought a calabash filled with the customary dish of rice, covered with a sauce made of stewed vegetables, peanuts, and a little meat. After one night at Sare Oura (my first in an African house [2]), we continued our journey southward on two borrowed bicycles; tied to the handlebars were several chickens given us by my assistant's family. Our destination was the village of Tonghia, which I had selected because the three hundred inhabitants were said to be mostly Badyaranké with few professing Moslems among them.

We arrived at Tonghia in the middle of a bright, clear, November morning. The long rainy season was recently over, the marshes below the village were green, and the men and women were in the fields gathering the last of the crops. We sat on a low wooden platform in front of the chief's house and waited for him to return from his labors. Children peeked from behind fences, an audience assembled in the courtyard, the tall and ancient chief arrived, and my assistant introduced me. He said that I was a student who had come to learn the language and observe the customs of the Badyaranké, and that I was hoping to become a teacher — as part of my education, I had come to Africa to learn how they live and work, and to write about them for others in America to read. The chief accepted this introduction, praised the motives, and gave us a tidy, thatch-roofed house in his compound. He ridiculed the bag of rice which I had brought, for rice was then abundant in his village. Tonghia proved to be a happy choice, and I passed the ensuing year in the chief's family, i.e.,

[2] Made of dried mud with bare earth floors, the houses are circular and have conical grass roofs and front and rear doorways. The inside is dark, and the main piece of furniture is a bed — sometimes manufactured and sometimes fashioned locally from bamboo.

5

with the persons living in his compound, and shared the food from his granaries.

The chief was named Niaboli Waliba; Niaboli is the family name inherited from his father, and Waliba is his personal name. He is one of the pioneers who left the village of Timbi in the forests of Northern Guinea around the turn of the last century to build a new village named Wassadou on the site known as Tonghia. Probably in his seventies, Waliba had been made chief twenty years before, and continues to work every day in his fields. Although his name is derived from the Arabic word for saint, Waliba is a pagan who relishes palm wine, honey beer, and Portuguese gin, and who is determined to finish his years without once praying to Allah.

My assistant's name was also Niaboli. He was a "nephew" of Waliba, not because of their common patronym, but because Waliba was his mother's "brother." Waliba was no close blood relation to the mother, but she, Waliba, and my assistant belong to a single matrilineal kinship grouping which shall be referred to as a matrisib.[3] Each Badyaranké belongs to the patronymic grouping of his father, of which there are eight in all, and to the matrisib grouping of his mother, of which there are at least twenty-six. My assistant and the chief, by coincidence, belonged to the same two groups.

During the bewildering and vivid first three weeks in the village, I learned to count and to respond properly to greetings, and having brought a chest of simple medicines, I quickly became familiar with the vocabulary of sickness. By the time my assistant returned to his duties in the Catholic school, I had gained some knowledge of Badyaranké kinship usages.

I had even been given a name. This came about when the blacksmiths of Tonghia learned that my patrilineal ancestors in New England had been blacksmiths for a number of generations. Despite their system of matrilineal descent, blacksmithing skills are

[3] The members of a matrisib include all persons who believe themselves to be related through common descent from an assumed but unknown ancestress. Descent is traced through females and not through males. One's mother and mother's mother belong to one's sib, but not one's father nor one's grandfather.

6

*Badyaranké villagers: top, a woman with freshly cut rice; bottom, an elder relaxing on his sitting platform.*

7

passed from father to son among the Badyaranké, and the craft is generally practiced by men of the patronym Kamara. (One's patronym is essential in greeting procedures: when passing someone on a path, you say, for example, "*Samio*," or "Good Morning," and the other responds by pronouncing your patronym.) After the discovery concerning my background, I was greeted throughout the countryside as "Kamara."

After my assistant's departure, I attempted to continue working alone, but with discouraging results. Eventually I learned of a fifteen-year-old boy in a nearby village who spoke French. He agreed to come to Tonghia as my interpreter, but unfortunately he proved to be a dismal investment. His own village had long been influenced by Islamized Manding culture, and he cared very little for his "conservative" relatives at Tonghia. Although he proved more or less adequate for the census-taking and genealogical inquiries occupying the second and third months of fieldwork, his efficiency span was exceedingly brief.

His most important contribution to my research was unsolicited. One morning I watched him splash some drops of liquid into his hands, lift a baseball cap which he usually wore, and rub the liquid over his head. When I asked what he was doing, he replied self-consciously that he was protecting himself from "the night people." His father had prepared a pink "medicine" to protect him from these individuals — conceivably anyone in the village — who are said to fly from their houses at night in eerie and unnatural forms to kill unsuspecting people. He explained that such "night people" see not only with ordinary eyes, but also with invisible eyes on their cheeks and on the backs of their heads, which are called "the eyes of the night." [4] Some even are said to possess eyes on the tips of their forefingers, which project beams resembling those of a flashlight. These creatures are supposed to revel ghoulishly in graves and to wear the clothing of the dead, acts considered repugnant by any self-respecting Badyaranké. My assistant conscientiously applied the liquid each morning and evening, and although it may have protected him from

[4] The Badyaranké phrase "of the night" means that the thing involved exists only in the invisible dimension of witchcraft.

"the night people," it did nothing to improve his value as an informant, and his employment was short lived.

At this point, I was tired of the diet of millet, rice, and sauce, weary of trying to express myself in a language that I barely understood, and eager to rediscover the cafes and movie houses of Dakar and to wear city clothes once again. During an interlude of two weeks in Dakar I not only indulged these yearnings for the amenities of city life, I also studied my notes and genealogies and formulated an outline of Badyaranké kinship nomenclature.

On my return trip to Tonghia I met a twenty-one-year-old Badyaranké youth from the village of Sunkutu in Guinea, who had been educated at French mission schools and had migrated north into Senegal to seek his fortune. He had studied for several years with the intention of entering the Catholic priesthood, but eventually cut himself loose from that calling, as well as from the interminable labors of village life. I discussed my rudimentary discoveries with him and persuaded him to return with me to the bush. Waliba provided him with an empty house in our compound, and he remained as my assistant for the following nine months.

My new assistant explained what he knew about the people who are said to fly at night to waste others' lives, but his was the testimony of a young man who had travelled and studied for several years. The subject of these night people made everyone so ill at ease that no one else wanted to discuss it, even privately. The Tonghia people were willing to explain their rituals and perform them in my presence, to explain the secret lore of male initiation, and to recite folktales for hours, but talk about the beings of the night sky elicited fear and silence. These creatures were so unpleasant and so terrifying that the people preferred not to talk about them. I was told that such beings had lived at Tonghia many years earlier, but had long since died; certain distant villages to the north and west were said to be presently infested with the creatures, but as far as Tonghia was concerned, "There are none here now."

By the end of May the torrid harmattan (a dust-laden wind that blows from the Sahara) had expended itself and the rains returned. Throughout the summer months the rain would fall several times during the week, and the men would be off, often alone, hoeing their fields from dawn until dusk. During these long, strenuous months the village was quiet and empty, and I spent many days lounging with three lonesome elders who were so bent from age that they could no longer work. They talked much about the early years of the village and the history of their compounds in particular. I also hiked to the fields and learned a great deal about the personal fears and thoughts of two adult men while in the solitude of their rain shelters. One elderly neighbor in an adjoining compound fell seriously ill during this season, and repeatedly sought me out to confide what he considered to be the causes of his illness, the omens and apparitions he had seen, and the dreams that haunted him. These hours of conversation in the shaded eaves of old men's houses, during showers in the fields, and in the nocturnal privacy of my own house enabled me to view the events of village life with more discerning eyes, eventually to appreciate why the chief's son fired on the owls, and to understand why my second assistant protected his body each morning with an application of pink "medicine."

## CHAPTER TWO

*Introducing*
*the Badyaranké*

## THE SETTING

The Badyaranké live in the flat savanna at the southern edge of the western Sudan, in a small region that overlaps into the Republic of Senegal, the Republic of Guinea, and Portuguese Guinea. Although they share their territory and often their villages with the Manding people (who call them Pajadinca) and various Fulani of the Casamance and Badiar regions, they are considered to be the most ancient inhabitants of their area. In all, some five thousand Badyaranké live today in approximately forty villages; less than half of these contain all or mostly Badyaranké inhabitants.

References to the Badyaranké in early nonscientific accounts were assembled and summarized by Monique Gessain in 1958; she did the first field research among them in the Guinean villages of Maru, Kutan, Paonka, Nemetaba, and Bagadat. Subse-

11

quent studies of their language,[1] social organization,[2] and religion [3] have helped this tiny and historically obscure people to emerge from anonymity. Their language has been classified by Joseph Greenberg as part of the Tenda subgroup of the West Atlantic family [4] and is thus related to that of the neighboring Coniagui and Bassari.

The country inhabited by the Badyaranké is greener and more lush at its southern limit in Guinea, and slightly drier with more dispersed vegetation at its northern extremity in Senegal. This is the country of the towering kapok tree, the stubby baobab, the mahoganies, a species of the gum tree known as *Daniella oliveri*, the oil palm, and the tall néré that produces large, edible pods. The wild forest animals include buffaloes, elands, antelopes, monkeys, elephants, lions, panthers, wild boars, hippopotami, crocodiles, and hyenas. Some diseases are prevalent: malaria carried by the mosquito, sleeping sickness by the tsetse fly, and schistosomiasis by the snail. The soil is usually hard, dry, and red from iron deposits. The landscape is characterized by numerous large red anthills and marshes along the banks of the meandering streams.

The year is divided into wet and dry seasons, with rain beginning toward the end of May, becoming most intense by August, and subsiding in November. During this time the streams swell and flood, travel is difficult, and mosquitoes make the night torture for man. During the months of December and January, the rain stops, but the countryside is still green, the nights are chilly, and the earth is fanned by strong easterly winds. The following months, however, become increasingly torrid with the hot, dry, dusty harmattan blowing out of the Sahara in the east until the eve of the rains; then the wind briefly reverses, the skies darken, the nights grumble with thunder, and the rains start to fall again.

Cereals cultivated by the Badyaranké include dry and wet rice, sorghum, several species of millets, and fonio. The vegetables con-

[1] Carreira 1963; Ducos 1964; Wilson 1959, 1961, 1965.
[2] Simmons 1967a.
[3] Simmons 1967b.
[4] 1963:8.

sist mainly of onions, tomatoes, beans, hot peppers, manioc, and gumbo. Peanuts are extensively cultivated and are the principal cash crop. Around the villages one finds mango, lime, and papaya trees, and occasionally banana; the several species of palm growing wild in the forest provide an ever-running source of palm wine. Domestic animals include cattle, sheep, goats, asses, dogs, cats, and chickens. In the streams are found catfish and a variety of smaller fish, as well as the giant python. Planting begins with the first rains early in June and work in the fields continues through the harvests, which begin as early as the last week of August for maize and terminate early in January when the rice is completely cut.

The Badyaranké of Portuguese Guinea have been Moslem for over a generation and for this reason have often been mistaken for the Manding people, who in this region have long been Islamized. The villages of Senegal, too, with the sole exception of Tonghia, are almost completely Islamized, and have been for at least two decades. Tonghia retains a considerable pagan population, but during the last ten years about half the inhabitants have abandoned their palm wine and begun to pray to Allah. In Guinea, notably at the village of Sunkutu, Islam has made some inroads, but otherwise the majority of the Badyaranké in Guinea continue their pagan ways, despite long familiarity with the Islamic Fulani [5] of the Fouta Djallon.

For a variety of reasons, I chose Tonghia in the *Arrondissement* of Bonconto as the site of my field investigation. Tonghia was a favored choice because many beliefs and practices of traditional Badyaranké society have eroded away in other Senegalese villages more influenced by Islam. The village was relatively pure from an ethnic point of view: of a total population in 1965 of 309 people, there were 6 Coniaguis and 2 Peul Fouta in residence. Tonghia was within bicycling distance of the Badyaranké villages of Sare Oura, Chafen, Mohum, Kantoro, Patin Kouta, and Paroumba, all of which I visited and three of which (Patin Kouta, Chafen, Sare Oura) became quite familiar to me.

[5] Also referred to as Peul or Fulbe; the Fulani from the Fouta Djallon are known as Peul Fouta or Poullo Fouta.

The French Catholic Fathers of Velingara in Senegal began a school at Tonghia in the late 1950s, but for a variety of reasons, the school was abandoned four years later, and in 1966 there was no school, no store, and no medical dispensary in the village. The nearest school and dispensary lie five miles away at the Fula Kunda village of Linkirring; the nearest administrative center, where taxes are paid and some disputes are settled, is at Bonconto, about ten miles distant; and the nearest market town, Velingara, is some forty miles to the north. In Velingara reside the Prefect, the local center of the Senegalese Government agricultural cooperative, and the French Catholic Fathers.

Tonghia was founded about sixty-five years ago by several Badyaranké families from the village of Timbi in northern Guinea. Niaboli Waliouae, a chief at Timbi, decided to move to the new site because of the hardships caused by the Fulani wars. For almost two decades the famous Fula Kunda chief, Moussa Molo, and the leader of the Peul Fouta, Alpha Yaya, had been making life uncomfortable for the smaller tribes lying in the paths of their holy wars. Niaboli Waliouae appealed to Moussa Molo to allow him to lead his people peacefully into the lands of the Fula Kunda where they could establish a new village. Moussa Molo approved, and the Tonghia people moved out of the contested forests of northern Guinea into the Casamance of Senegal.

## THE MATRISIB

Badyaranké society is organized into at least twenty-six named matrilineal descent groups (*catyi*) to be referred to as matrisibs, following usages by Robert Lowie [6] and George Murdock.[7] A child belongs forever to the matrisib of his mother, and a child born of a Badyaranké father and a mother from a patrilineal society such as the Fulani or Manding belongs to no sib until he is formally adopted into one of these twenty-six groups. The matrisibs are dispersed rather than localized, and no territories are associated with them; there are no myths or recollections concerning which matrisib is oldest, nor how or where the groups originated. Most,

6 1920: 111.
7 1960:47.

| Sib name | Totem | Joking partner |
| --- | --- | --- |
| Unioké-Udiare | ? | Ukamara |
| Biyantian-Bisambuad | elephant | Ukamara |
| Irar-Bukor | bear | Uranyi-Usambi |
| Farancamityi-Udiou | hyena | Damanton-Congatyi |
| Usambi-Bisambuad | hare | Ukamara-Bukor ? |
| Ufafa-Burong | ? | Binyassi-Busae |
| Kamancuta-Bisimbon | lizard | Bunasia |
| Binantio-Bubare | boar | ? |
| Binyaourundi | ? | Buratyi |
| Ukamara-Bukor | python | ? |
| Damanton-Congatyi ? | chicken, python | Farancamityi-Udiou |
| Uranyi | lion, panther | Irar-Bukor |
| Bunasia | boar | Kamancuta-Bisimbon |
| Buratyi | python | Binyaourundi |

* Table 1 includes all paired combinations of sibs and corresponding sibs of joking partners.

but not all, matrisibs possess animal totems, referred to as "my mother's brother," which are never killed or eaten by the respective members, but otherwise serve no further manifest purpose. Most matrisibs are allied with one other matrisib to form exogamous pairs, and of such pairs their members say: "We are the same thing; we are as one matrisib." For example, those in the matrisib Binyassi say that they are the same as the Busae, and the Biyantian say that they are identical to the Bisambuad (see Table 1). Such pairs are exogamous, observe the same totemic taboos, and act as a single corporation in widow inheritance.[8] The exogamous bipartite matrisibs are said to have originated from fission due to quarrels in the very distant past. The following fables illustrate what is known of the genesis of these paired descent groups.

There were two siblings, both Binyassi, who went to gather the pods of the néré tree. The younger sibling climbed up to pick and handed them to the older brother below. The older brother on the ground gave

[8] When a man dies, his widow is inherited by another man in his sib, who becomes her husband; members of the deceased husband's sib are responsible for taking care of her, and she is wedded to that sib until her death. Badyaranké are polygamous.

them away to anyone who passed by. The brother in the tree said, "Don't give them away. What is there left for me?" The older brother continued to give them away. The younger brother said, "If you continue, I'll kick you," and the older brother said, "Go ahead." The younger tried but fell and broke his foot. After that incident, he with the broken foot is Busae, and he who is generous is Binyassi.

Two brothers, both of the matrisib Biyantian, went fishing. The smaller brother caught the biggest fish and hid them. When they finished, the older brother saw that the younger had more than he. The older brother asked why the younger had more, and he said, "Because I am more intelligent." He thereafter became known as Bisambuad.

Once the Farancamityi all had the same mother and this mother died. It was necessary to divide up her clothes. One person wanted to divide evenly, and the other said, "No; we are more numerous and want the biggest part." He became known as Udiou.

No Badyaranké sib has ever divided within living memory, and their divisions may be assumed to be static and probably ancient. Not everyone agrees, however, as to which matrisibs derived from which. Many Usambi, for example, insist that they are paired with the Bisambuad in an exogamous bond, with the hare as their totem. Some Bisambuad deny this and claim links to the Biyantian, with the elephant as totem. All combinations known are listed in Table 1, with their corresponding totemic species. I have been told that the partners in such pairs vary in the Badyaranké villages of Portuguese Guinea, which may explain the origin of ideas concerning alternative alignments. Although the matrisibs are without a territorial locus, the ways in which they are combined vary from one region to another.

In addition to the eleven or more exogamous, paired matrisibs, there are also five which are undifferentiated. The undivided descent group is referred to by the same term as the divided descent group (catyi). The genealogical links within the matrisib are never completely known, and there exists no lesser grouping within the matrisib that could be described as a lineage, and no fusion of sibs into phratries. Aside from its bipartite structure, the matrisib neither divides into smaller units nor combines into larger ones.

Kinship to others in one's matrisib is assumed, ancestors are forgotten above one ascending generation, and there is neither knowledge of, nor concern for, distant or original ancestors. The matrisib possesses no permanent ancestral shrine and no communal burial plot.

Each of the matrisibs, with a few exceptions, identifies with a wild species of quadruped which is considered to be the mother's brother (*mbani*) of the respective members, and is never killed or eaten by them. No identity of character is assumed between the matrisib and its animal relations; those related to the lion, for example, do not believe themselves to be more ferocious than those related to the chicken.

## JOKING RELATIVES

Most matrisibs, whether undivided or bipartite, are reciprocally allied to one other sib to form a relationship named for a word from Manding, *sunaho*.[9] For example, the people of matrisib Buratyi are joking partners with the Binyaourundi, and members of the bipartite sib Binyassi-Busae are joking partners with the Ufafa-Burong (Table 1). Knowledge of genealogical links between joking partners is irrelevant, and the relationship has no implications for marriage. Not everyone agrees, however, as to which sib should be aligned to which, and there is even some variation in alignment from village to village. I recorded two complaints by men whose sunaho had taken meat without permission from ritual sacrificial offerings, and several references to partners who had asked their reciprocals for trifling sums of money and had been refused, all in good humor. In any case, the joking relationship is neither conspicuous nor important among the Badyaranké, and is certainly an incomplete adaptation of a Manding custom. It allows members of the opposed matrisibs to associate in a spirit of familiarity that sometimes ignores formalities based on relative age, wealth, sex, or the gravity of serious occasions.

## THE PATRONYM

Despite universal membership in matrisibs, each Badyaranké bears the "name of salutation" (*kopanyi*) of his father. He is never addressed by the name of his matrisib. The "names of salutation"

---

[9] Labouret 1934:101–104.

pass from fathers to their sons and daughters, and hereafter will be referred to as patronymics. A Badyaranké's name consists first of his patronymic (there are only eight: Banaro, Bandia, Boumbali, Kamara, Niaboli, Nioké, Sané, Sandé), and a personal name that need not be sex-limited. If a woman bears children by someone other than her legitimate husband, these children will bear the patronymic of their pater. If the pater dies while the children are very young and his wife and children are inherited by a man with a patronymic different from the deceased, the children may be addressed by the name of their new father. The patronymic is inherited from the mother's legal husband as a reflection of sociological paternity, and from the mother's common-law husband to give the appearance of legitimacy. The patronymics entail no norms of exogamy, have no totems, and although there is no expressed rule, tend to be localized because of a preference for patrilocal residence. On no occasion, ritual or mundane, do people of the same patronymic unite for collective action. The patronymics form an independent system from the matrisibs, and contrast with them in the eight respects listed in Table 2.

TABLE 2  CONTRASTS OF THE MATRISIB AND PATRONYMIC

| Matrisib | Patronymic |
| --- | --- |
| Name not used in address or reference | Name used in address and reference |
| Fateful, derives from the mother | Contractual, depends on the pater |
| Marriage prohibited between members | Marriage permitted between members |
| Residentially dispersed | Residentially localized |
| Totemic observances | Non-totemic |
| Possesses a collective ritual (*padunko*) | No ritual |
| Matrilineal | Patrilineal |
| Members consider themselves to be related by kinship | Not a kinship or corporate unit |

If a man's several wives derive from different matrisibs, the children of each union will belong to the mother's respective sib but all the children will bear the father's patronymic. The

18

Badyaranké believe that both parents contribute materially to pro-
creation, and that "blood and bones" derive from them both. To
my question, "Whence comes the soul?" the Badyaranké only
laughed and reassured me that it comes from God (*Kodan*).
There is a feeling that siblings who come from the same "stomach"
are closer; in the idiom, *stomach* may mean the same mother or
the same matrisib.

KIN TERMS AND BEHAVIOR

The Badyaranké kin terms and the categories of people to which
they refer (for a male speaker) are described below.

| | |
|---|---|
| *Nna* | refers to all women of one's matrisib in the generation above ego, including the biological mother. |
| *Mbani* | refers to all males of one's matrisib in the generation above ego, including the mother's full brothers. |
| *Dyasé* | includes all males and females of one's matrisib, of one's own generation, who are older than ego. |
| *Nmpiaré* | includes all males and females of one's matrisib, of one's own generation, who are younger than ego. |
| *Nimé* | refers to all males and females of one's matrisib who belong to the generation below ego; i.e., the offspring of all female dyasé or nmpiaré. |
| *Numbé* | applies to all children of all men of one's matrisib, including one's own children. |
| *Nitia* | refers to the offspring of one's numbé. |
| *Ape* | refers to all men of the matrisib to which one's own mother has married, including one's own father. |
| *Mbinki* | includes all women of the matrisib into which one's own mother has married. The children of mbinki are thus mbinki if female, and *ape*, if male. |
| *Fadi* | refers to all children of men known as *ape*, through women who are not of one's matrisib. The children of the father's second wife or the children of the father's brother would thus be fadi. |
| *Niaé* | refers to all wives of all men of one's matrisib, including one's own wife. This term is used by both male and female speakers: one's female siblings (dyasé or nmpiaré) refer to one's wife as "my wife." |
| *Mame* | refers to the nna or *ape* of one's own nna or mbani. It may also refer to the immediate parents of one's *ape*, and to one's ancestors. |

*19*

For people living together, these terms allow transient and contextual usages. All of one's father's wives are called nna, but if they are not of one's own matrisib, their children will be called fadi. If a co-mother (not one's own mother) divorces one's father, she ceases to be nna. Similarly, a male not of one's father's matrisib who marries a woman known as nna will be called *ape* as long as the marriage endures.

Along with these categories of kin, there are set patterns of behavior between the categories. The father prescribes the work his son does, and has the right to insult or hit the son if he is disobedient. The relationship of a son to his father is constrained, in that the son does not joke with the father or insult him, nor does he talk of sexual exploits. A son would not use his father's personal name in address, but a father always calls his son by name. Nevertheless, the economic and emotional bond of a father to his son is stronger than that of a mother's brother to his sister's son (mbani-nimé). A son fears his father more than any other relative; however, if a father insults or abuses his wife, her son might insult and perhaps threaten the father. No money is lent between fathers and sons; fathers may not appropriate their son's money without consent. The father decides whether or not one of his young sons should be loaned to a childless or destitute mother's brother.

A father is responsible for finding his son a wife. Although the mother's brother may be asked to find his sister's son a wife, he is less obligated to deliver. The skills of blacksmithing, weaving, and hunting are transmitted through the father. The father must pay taxes to the government for his young sons and unbetrothed daughters, provide kola nuts for the naming of his children, and seek clothing, fees, regalia, and food for his son's or daughter's initiation ceremonies (circumcision or excision). A father, or more probably a brother, could be called upon to fill in for a young man who owes a day's work to his prospective in-laws. A son, once he begins to clear his own fields and engage in wage labor, is expected to present frequent gifts of money, and such commodities as clothing, beds, and storage trunks to his father.

If a man has been living and working with his father, he should inherit most of the treasures at his father's demise. The oldest son always inherits the largest share; the preferred inheritors are son, brother, and finally sister's son. A man generally leaves his fields, crops, gun, tools, sheep, goats, cattle, mango trees, jewelry, clothing, amulets, and money to his sons. However, although it is considered disrespectful for a son to wear the garments of his deceased father, this is often done. Of twenty-eight separate inheritances of rice plots at Tonghia, eighteen passed directly in the agnatic line through men. Use rights of plots in eight cases were passed from father to daughter. In one instance, a man inherited from his mother's brother, and in another instance, from his mother's father. Thus, rice plots, although used by women, are generally passed from father to son. A woman loses rights in her husband's plot if she divorces him. Sons and daughters are expected to provide a sheep or goat for their father's funeral sacrifice.

A father is said to be more affectionate to his daughter than to his son. He may strike his daughter for exceptional disobedience, but this is rare. A daughter may inherit some money and, occasionally, a sheep or even a mango tree from her father. She loses rights to her father's rice plot when she marries.

One's father's sister is not the object of unusual or circumspect behavior on the part of a male. He may bring her a gift of cereal at harvest time, and in an earlier era, the boy was expected to supply her with firewood. He uses the term *mbinki* to address her. Although he might contribute an animal to her funeral sacrifice, she is unimportant to him from the point of view of inheritance, since this would generally be left to others. It is said that the father's sister is easy to marry and for that reason is the preferred marriage partner. A father might procure his matrisib sisters for his son with fewer conditions and complications.

A brother should consider his older brother with affection and deference, although their relationship is informal enough so that they address each other by name. The younger brother is customarily blamed for any quarrel he might have with his senior, and is punished accordingly by the father. If several brothers live and work together, the most junior is sent as a seasonal wage laborer into Wolof country; [10] the usual arrangement is that he render as much as half of his earnings to the older brothers who have remained at home to care for the family fields. Borrowing takes place most frequently between brothers, especially between those who reside in the same compound or village. Brothers frequently substitute for each other in the performance of bride services.[11] A brother may inherit the wives of his deceased full brother by virtue of their common membership in the matrisib. Instances of serious quarrels are rare between brothers, and the one observed case concerned the inheriting of a woman.

A woman's behavior toward her female siblings is less formal. She may offer frequent gifts such as onions, hot peppers, and various other vegetables to her senior and junior sisters. She may also distribute a small portion of her half of her daughter's bride-wealth to her brothers and sisters. It is not rare for a young man to confide his money with an older sister, nor is it rare for a married woman to contribute to the clothing and ceremonial requirements of a young brother, especially if their father is old. Full sisters are forbidden to marry the same individual, or even to marry two full brothers.

A half sibling (fadi) is always on less intimate terms with one than a sibling of the same matrisib. Theoretically he should not inherit one's wives or possessions, but it does occasionally happen, when the full brother is young, dead, or disinterested. If a half sibling lives in the compound and has helped the deceased to earn his living, then he should be favored over a more distant matrisib relative. Children of the same father feel a certain solidarity, although it is less strong than that between the sons of one mother. This behavior is expressed in marriage preference when it is said that the father's sister is easiest to marry, and after her, the daughter of a half sibling.

The mother is the most trusted of all relatives, and the one most concerned with the children's welfare. For a Badyaranké, there is no insult more serious than to one's mother. A child

---

[10] The area inhabited by the neighboring Wolof tribe to the north, extending from Dakar to Tambacounda.

[11] Work performed for the father of the prospective bride before marriage.

sleeps with its mother during the first two years of its life and is subsequently sent elsewhere, generally to a matrilineal relative of either parent; here the child may remain for one or two months, or perhaps for several years, to "forget its mother's breast." Married daughters often return to their mother to give birth or to convalesce when they or their children are ailing. A daughter is said never to borrow from her mother, although she might from her father. Young men entrust their money and valuables to be kept in their mother's large earthen urn where her own valuables are stored. A lad frequently borrows petty cash from his mother to purchase tobacco and kola nuts. A young man gives part of his earnings to his mother and may eventually support her in old age. Sons often pay their mother's taxes, pay for her cotton to be woven into cloth, and give her gifts of cloth, kolas, and tobacco. It is said that a son has more affection for his mother, and a daughter more affection for her father, because parents and children of the same sex do not work together.

When a woman dies, she generally forfeits use rights in her rice, peanut, and fonio fields, all of which tend to belong to her husband. A woman's treasures amount to rubber sandals, a few kerchiefs, some bracelets and rings, a modest couple of baskets filled with cloth, a pot, mosquito netting, uncombed cotton, needles, and occasionally two or three sheep or goats. Both sons and daughters may inherit these goods, and generally the son takes the livestock, leaving the feminine goods to the women. Invariably the largest portion of a woman's effects go to other women of her matrisib. Her son is expected to give one or possibly several animals for her funeral sacrifice.

Although it is less serious to insult one's mother's brother (mbani) than to insult one's mother, a Badyaranké does not like to hear his mbani's name abused. Senior citizens remember that an individual previously contributed more to his mbani's welfare and expected to inherit more of his fortune than is the practice today. A mother's brother may request the services of his nimé, but he can exercise no sanction if refused.

If a boy has no father, or if his mother's bride price was never paid, he may live with the mother's brother, and be treated as a

23

son from the point of view of labor, discipline, and inheritance. If the child is female, and if the mother's bridewealth was never paid, the mother's brother can take all bridewealth from his nimé's marriage, for children born out of wedlock are the mother's brother's responsibility.

The wife of one's mother's brother or the wife of any other male of one's matrisib is referred to as "my wife," and her children are "my children." One may inherit any wife of a deceased male in one's matrisib, and all their unmarried children. The Badyaranké say that "it is not serious to be caught sleeping with the wife of mother's brother," and one frequently hears of such events. When the mother's brother dies, the sister's son also inherits his debts. Often a mother's brother will contribute a sheep or goat to the funeral sacrifice of his uterine nephews and nieces, and vice versa.

In address, one calls the mother's brother by the term *mbani*, but the reciprocal *nimé* is seldom used. The older man will often address his nimé as mbani to indicate affection and esteem.

MARRIAGE

A Badyaranké father is responsible for representing a young man in his search for a wife. If the prospective father-in-law accepts three successive gifts of kolas and palm wine, the way is open for serious discussion of financial arrangements which result in the son becoming committed to from three to six years of gift-giving, labor, and money payments. The goods he contributes generally include yearly payments of money, salt, and bamboo mats, in addition to clothing for the girl. Each year he will be expected to pay her Government taxes (550 francs, or $2.20) and to assemble a group of young men to devote one or sometimes two full days of work in the fields of his prospective father-in-law. During these years the young man visits his betrothed's compound often to help with such tasks as roof-thatching, house-building, and fence-mending, and to bring gifts of kola nuts, tobacco, and palm wine. If the youth is a blacksmith, he will forge tools without charge for the girl's father, mother, brothers, sisters, and perhaps one or two of her other matrisib relatives in the village.

24

Bridewealth is received by the girl's father, who divides it equally with his wife. The wife in turn may give some small amount to some of her matrisib relatives, although she is under no obligation to do so. The father keeps nothing, however, if he never completed bridewealth for his own wife. The final marriage payment includes a robe, a bull, and mosquito net for the father, a marmite and clothing for the girl, and (if the girl is a virgin) a cow for her and her mother.

Bridewealth totals tend to be forgotten and exaggerated. But my survey found that, including the value of livestock and money payments, bridewealth payments of 23 men ranged from 13,000 to 60,000 francs ($52 to $240), with a mean approximating 33,300 francs ($133.20). Such payments are substantial, since the mean of 33,300 francs represents about two years of peanut earnings for the average man.

A most striking regularity of marriage preference is shown in the high frequency of village endogamy. In 94 out of 122 marriages (77 percent), both partners were natives of Tonghia. In 1965, all 24 eligible unmarried girls in the village had been spoken for by Tonghian young men; thus not one girl of the next generation of young wives will leave. No norm states it is better to marry a girl from the same village, but the Badyaranké feel it is more desirable to have a son-in-law who is nearby and available because of all the goods and services he can provide during the years of service.

The Badyaranké claim that it is "easier" to marry the father's sister (mbinki). Thirty-one of a sample of 118 marriages (26 percent) actually fulfill this preference. In 7 of these 31 marriages for which information is complete, the bridewealth payments were below the mean for the entire sample, suggesting that marriage with a father's sister (mbinki) may be slightly less costly. A father, by arranging this type of marriage for his son, can provide dependable income for some women of his own matrisib and ensure its perpetuation through his son's children. This union provides additional security for the bride who moves into a compound where her husband's father is also her mother's brother. Although there is a stated preference for marriage with

25

mbinki, there is no norm of this formula (men of matrisib X prefer to marry women of matrisib Y), and thus no recurrent and continuing affinal alliances of matrisibs.

The term for wife-giver (*biton*, i.e., "in-law") applies to the wife's mother, brother, sister, and any other member of her matrisib who is close to the girl genealogically or residentially, or who is eligible to receive part of the bridewealth. The wife-taker (*bitondin*, i.e., "little in-law") refers to all men and women of the husband's matrisib. Since all of a man's full brothers, mother's brothers (mbani), and sister's sons (nimé) may inherit his wife, she is referred to as "my wife" by all of them.

The Badyaranké practice no in-law avoidances. Once the bridewealth is paid and the girl has moved to the husband's compound, her father no longer expects the lad to work for him. The bride is given a bed in the collective women's house by the headman of her husband's compound. After one week of ceremonial adjustments she takes up her duties of cooking, washing, and cultivating, and sleeps with her husband.

In turn, a husband provides agricultural land for his wife, pays her taxes, provides for her clothing, and continually gives her little gifts of kolas, tobacco, and ornaments. These expenditures for three men, each with one wife, amounted to 3, 12, and 15 percent of their respective annual earnings. When a wife dies, her husband is expected to contribute to the funeral sacrifice, and in the event of his death, her father is expected to do the same.

Thus, bridewealth secures the labor and sexual services of a particular woman to her husband's matrisib for the duration of her lifetime, except in the event of divorce. Furthermore, it ensures that the husband's matrisib will benefit from all the labor of her sons and half the bridewealth from her daughters.

DIVORCE

If a husband terminates a marriage, his wife returns to her mother, and her bridewealth is not returned to him. Any children, too, go with their mother. Once a woman has produced a child, she may leave without any consequences, but the child must remain with her husband. If a woman dies shortly after marriage, the bereaved husband can claim nothing.

*Women at work:* top, *preparing the evening rice;* bottom, *repairing a gourd bowl.*

If, however, a wife abandons her husband before she has borne children, the bridewealth must be returned to him by her father; in such a case, even the value of the yearly work parties is claimed. Her father probably would assemble this money for payment to the first husband when she remarries. Never would the former father-in-law provide another woman to the first husband; also never would he arrange the marriage of two daughters to a single individual, or even to two brothers. The proscription against sororal polygyny tends to create as many separate affinal bonds as there are daughters. From the point of view of the number of individuals he can command for labor, gifts, and money, it is to the father's advantage that these ties not be redundant.

Since a woman generally owns no land, she must forfeit use rights in her husband's land if she leaves him; secondly, she must forfeit her children if she takes the initiative for divorce. Thus, despite the hypothetical fragility of marriage in matrilineal societies, marriage is stable, and only 17 of 107 marriages (15.89 percent) at Tonghia ended in divorce. Compared to divorce rates among the matrilineal Cewa [12] and Ndembu,[13] marriage is comparatively stable among the Badyaranké.

The reasons for these 17 divorces include five cases of women who were attracted to other men, three of women who were abandoned by their husbands, one of an allegedly impotent husband, one of a wife who was insane, one of a wife who suspected the other co-wife of bewitching her son, and one of a wife who argued with a co-wife over cooking matters. Quarrels between co-wives are not conspicuously frequent despite the fact that nearly one-third of all marriages are polygynous.

THE COMPOUND

The elementary domestic group of Badyaranké society is the dependent polygynous extended family, or compound. To create a compound, a man first builds two primary structures: the headman's house (*bellibu*) for himself to the east, and the women's house (*bumba*) for all his wives and their infant children

12 Marwick 1965a:173.
13 Turner 1964:62.

to the west. Boys leave the women's house when they reach the
age of about four years to share their father's quarters or to sleep
in a third house constructed for their use. Girls remain with their
mothers in the women's house until marriage. When the sons
marry, they build their own houses to the north and south of the
axis between the two primary structures, thus creating a ring
with the solitary women's house to the west, and the men's houses
closing the circle to the east. The sons' wives move into the
collective women's house with their co-wives, mothers-in-law, and
the wives of other male residents.

In the open area in the middle of the compound stands a
wooden post, at the base of which, to the east, lies a circle of
stones where the younger men and boys eat in the evening. In
front of each house the men build a sitting platform which is
sometimes roofed. In front of the women's house there is a pro-
fusion of roofless sitting platforms — one for each woman who

FIGURE 2    COMPOUND OF NIABOLI WALIBA, CHIEF OF TONGHIA

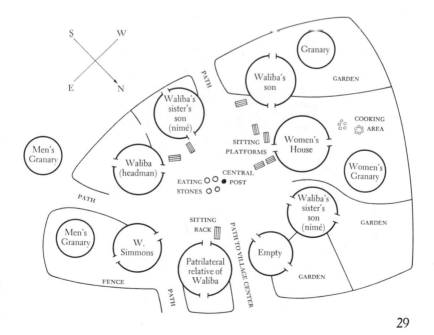

Top, *path leading to the tree at the village center;* bottom, *women at work in front of their collective house.*

lives there. Cooking and mortaring of parched grain are done within the women's house during the rainy months and to the rear of the house during the dry season. In back of the men's houses are elevated granaries, a washing area, and enclosed gardens of tomatoes, manioc, or peppers. The dead are also buried within the compound. Men are buried underneath or to the rear of their houses, and women are buried behind their collective house. The corpse, either male or female, is interred on its right side facing east, and follows the living arrangement of men to the east and women to the west. The entire compound is usually contained within a woven grass fence five feet high.

The Badyaranké say men live to the east of the women because life began in the east and because the prevailing wind blows from east to west. The wind causes the "breath" and "heat" of the women to blow away from the men; Badyaranké believe the men exposed to these exhalations would suffer vague illnesses. The combined smoke, heat, and exhalations of the women in their noisy chamber bear mystical danger, the men say, and this is why the women's house is built of reeds, to ventilate this impurity. Male informants also say that if a woman resided for any length of time in a man's house, her presence would cause the walls to crack and the house to collapse. Thus, Badyaranké men live dispersed toward the favored east, upwind from the noisy, breathing, burning women.

Compounds bear the personal names of their male founders (Candania, meaning "at Dania's") or the patronymic of their male founder (Sandé Kunda, "the place of the Sandé"), or sometimes even the name of a conspicuous tree growing near the compound (Cambiae, "at the néré tree"). The largest number of dwellings in any one compound at Tonghia was twelve, and the smallest two, with a mean of six dwellings for the total population of fifteen compounds.

Residents are recruited into the compounds according to several rules, the most general of which is the preference by sons to reside patrilocally and for women to reside virilocally after marriage. So, as a rule, men remain and women leave unless, as occasionally happens, the parties to the marriage derive from the

31

same compound. There are other, more specific rules for recruit-ment. A girl's father may request his prospective son-in-law to reside uxorilocally during the years prior to marriage while the young man is accumulating bridewealth and performing services for the girl's family. If a man's father has died and the compound has dispersed, he is free to move in with a man who is the terminological equivalent of his father, or with a brother, or even with a mother's brother. The death of a man with wives and children offers them two alternatives: first, the women and their children may go to the compounds of their respective inheritors; second, if the deceased was a headman or if he had several wives with sons needed in the labor force of the compound, an inheritor might be invited to move to the compound to replace the de-ceased, thus necessitating a minimum of change. Finally, an old woman whose husbands have died may return to her sons or daughters to pass her remaining years under their care.

The first and most inclusive rule favors patrilocal residence. Given a variety of conditions contingent on occurrences of death, sterility, dispersion, and migration, avunculocal and neolocal resi-dence may also be desirable. A sample of fifty-four married men living at Tonghia shows 52 percent residing in compounds where their fathers live or had lived before death, or in com-pounds with a father's brother, a father's nimé, or a more at-tenuated patrilateral relation. Approximately 11 percent of the married men reside in the compounds of their mother's brothers.

If a man's wives belong to different matrisibs, as they generally do, their respective families will be matrilineally unrelated. When the sons marry, and the third generation matures, this compound will be composed of a large number of men who bear the patro-nym of a single male founder, but who belong to numerous matrisibs. If a compound was established by two brothers, in this case the third generation would be even more diversely and tenuously related.

Sometimes a headman's matrisib relations (i.e., his dyasé, mbani, nmpiaré, or nimé) choose to move into his compound; this di-vides his loyalties between his own sons and these men. Bad-yaranké say that a man whose nimé and numbé live together in a single compound expects dissension. One son in such a family complained repeatedly that he had worked for many years to support his father and that the father's nimé had come to live on their prosperity. Another grumbled that his father was less demanding of his sib relatives, and that the nimé flatter the headman but neglect obligations to others in the compound. In such a situation the nimé may complain that the headman's sons resent them, or they may suspect that the sons envy their privileged relationship with the headman. One such nimé protested bitterly that his headman's wives favored their own sons when they cooked and distributed the evening meal.

Discontented factions are always stirring beneath the surface in populous compounds. Diverse matrilineal loyalties, jealousies between kinsmen, and suspicions of real and supposed neglect of communal labors weigh behind the day-to-day amenities of eating and working together. A Badyaranké proverb states that "many feet are needed in a compound to prevent the weeds from taking over." But I was told also by Waliba that people must quarrel if they are to live together; quarreling alone does not cause a family to disintegrate for it is an inevitable consequence of communal life. One young man told me that families collapse and disperse because of those people who become nocturnal beasts, those whom my second informant described as "the night people."

## THE HEADMAN

The headman should be the eldest permanent male resident willing and competent to perform the responsibilities involved. A man is always head of the compound that he took the initiative to build. Since the important prerequisite for headmanship is competent old age, the question of succession involves kinship in only a derivative sense. The status of headman may pass to a son, a brother, a sister's son, or an unrelated person, depending on who is living in the compound. Although the position is desired and respected, succession is not a controversial issue.

Within the compound, the headman takes responsibility for the collective fields (*marouba*) and decides which days of the week the men will work for their collective interests. He is ultimately responsible for the delegation of tasks among the women and arbitrates when the women disagree about how various tasks should be done. He hears and settles arguments between male residents of his compound, which usually concern real or suspected neglect of collective labors. Although his voice is important, he is not immune to rebuke, and not infrequently the younger men will argue vociferously if they find his criticism unjustified or his judgment faulty. The following episode between Chief Niaboli Waliba and his sister's son Tunkan certainly echoes similar loud exchanges heard in Badyaranké compounds for centuries.

Waliba was angry because the men were going to the fields without their digging tools. Tunkan said, "Leave them alone; they know how to work. You're never content with their work." Waliba asked, "Why do you say that? I don't go spy on the fields. I don't know what you do there. How can I be malcontent?" Tunkan said, "You are malcontent." Waliba replied, "Now you are responsible. You don't want me to talk. You contradict all that I say. You go ahead and command." Tunkan answered, "All that concerns the work let us do. All you have to do is tell us what to do. How we do it is for us to decide." Waliba shouted, "I give you all my powers, the compound, the village, the chieftainship, everything!"

The headman's duties are varied. He is custodian of the collective fields and granaries, the seed for the following year, and the packet of magical roots that one mixes with seed on planting day. He determines the dates of the first sowing and of the harvests. It is his responsibility to buy meat for the compound and to divide the meat into appropriate portions for the men and women. Surplus dried meat and fish are smoked and stored in his house. The headman buys the yearly supply of salt for the compound, guards the sacks of salt in his house, and metes it out as the women require. The fruit of the néré pod is powdered by the women and stored in his house until needed for feeding infants and children. The young men of the compound contribute to their headman's welfare, especially if he is too old to work, with gifts of money and clothing. When the younger men buy palm wine, Portuguese gin, kola nuts, or tobacco, they customarily give some to the headman. In former years, when the young men's work group (*palau*) labored in the collective field of a compound, the headman would reward the members with a quantity of millet.

Formerly, each compound had a continuing arrangement with a family of smiths to provide it with iron tools: the headman would furnish iron for the smiths, the smiths would supply the labor, and the headman would reward them at the end of each harvest with a gift of millet or corn. The practice of yearly gifts of grain continues in irregular and diminished form, but the headman no longer supplies the iron and many individuals frequent several smiths on a cash-and-carry basis.

Another aspect of compound life centers around the headman: water for the compound is carried from the spring by women and stored in pottery jars under the eaves of the headman's house. At the bottom of these jars they place pebbles, said to have come from God (Kodan) "by lightning." These pebbles protect those who drink the water against lightning and against any genies (*dyinné*) that might desire to consume the family water. Another protective item is required when a new compound has been constructed: the headman buys an appropriate medicine (*sada*) from a marabout, and the sada when buried under the central post is said to procure health, abundance, and fertility for the compound's inhabitants.

## DIVISION OF LABOR IN THE COMPOUND

The men work on an average of three days a week in the collective corn and millet fields of the compound, and on the remaining days they rest, work their own private fields, or help in someone else's field. Every man and post-adolescent boy owns a peanut field, the crop of which provides the only important source of cash in the village, other than trifling sales of seeds, mangoes, or beeswax to chance passersby. Some men find it necessary to plant private corn and millet fields to feed their many children, to entertain guests, or to feed workers contracted to clear or hoe their private fields. Thus, the men of a compound form a corporation only with respect to their collective fields, which

35

are worked by whoever lives there, under the custodianship of the headman.

The women possess no collective fields, but cultivate individual rice plots which, in most cases, belong to their husbands. The wives of one man occasionally work a rice plot together and store their yield in a single granary (a big vessel made of clay mixed with straw), but more frequently a woman works her plot alone or with a daughter. Peanuts and fonio are planted yearly by most women, usually in fallow fields belonging to their husbands. Men reside in separate houses but cultivate together, whereas the women live together but work apart. Millet and corn are raised by men and stored in a single collective granary; rice and fonio are raised by women and stored in private urns.

Although the headman acts as custodian of the men's granary, a young boy is usually responsible for allocating corn and millet to the women for cooking. He is considered less likely to be influenced than a mature man might be by the demands of the women who, presumably, would take all the grain if they could. The women provide their own rice, vegetables, and peanuts, so every meal consists of both male and female contributions. If a man has two wives, the senior wife cooks for the compound in the morning, and the junior at night. The morning cooking chore is easier and more desirable because the temperature is cooler and the cook is not tired from her day's work in the fields.

For example, in a compound consisting of three married men — A, B, and C —each with two wives, the elder wife of A would cook one morning, the elder wife of B would cook the second morning, and the elder wife of C the third morning. The same procedure would be followed by the younger wives for the evening meal. In another example, if a man's wives are middle-aged and younger women abound in the compound, both of the elder women may work on alternate mornings, leaving all the evening cooking to the younger women. Aged and decrepit women are free from all responsibilities of cooking.

Often the partition of morning and evening tasks between the women becomes complicated. In the compound of Niaboli Wa-

36

Top, *man weeding his millet field*; bottom, *a mother and her child.*

liba live three young wives — Alarba, Bintadyo, and Nani — who are approximately the same age and the sole wives of Sanaba, Karfo, and Tunkan, respectively. Alarba was forced to retire from work for several days because of a miscarriage. Her morning cooking role was assumed by Bintadyo. When Alarba recovered, she chose to cook in the evening and Bintadyo continued in the morning. Karfo, Bintadyo's husband, told Waliba that he did not want his wife to cook in the morning because Tunkan was his senior in years, and for that reason Tunkan's wife Nani should be given the morning tasks. Tunkan bellowed: "So it is only now that you realize that I am older. Hah." Nani was told to do the morning cooking; she refused, however, and said that when her husband took a second wife, she would willingly take the morning meal. Alarba also said that she did not want to resume in the morning at Bintadyo's expense — each trying to be polite and forego the easier task. So after much discussion, Waliba decreed that all three should work alternately on morning and evening meals, and that is what they did.

A woman cooks her own stores of rice and fonio, but each time she prepares it in sufficient quantity for the entire compound, as do the other women in their turn. Thus, food from the collective men's granary enters the cooking pots by way of redistribution, whereas the women's cooking, labor, and grain are exchanged serially from day to day. If, for some reason, a woman refuses to cook one day, the others may refuse in their turn, until all have refused. The headman has no powers of coercion in such cases, and it can happen that the residents of a compound do without supper for several days until all the women have had their turn at being idle.

The morning meal is brought to the fields during the growing season and is eaten in the village during the dry months. When in the village the men breakfast together in the headman's house or on his sitting rack, and the women eat in or in front of their dwelling. In the evening the headman dines in front of his house, generally with a young boy or another old man. The younger men and boys have their meal seated at the ring of stones in the center of the compound. The women eat the evening meal in front of their house on the sitting racks. The eldest woman generally shares her bowl of food with a young girl; all the others eat together out of only two or three bowls, even including several wives of one man. On no occasion do men and women take a meal together in the same house.

On the days a woman sleeps with her husband, she washes his clothing, sweeps his house, and brings his water supply. A man generally passes three successive nights with each wife, regardless of her age or appearance. Older women tend to withdraw from this privilege and sleep regularly in the collective house, where they act as guardians. In the center of the women's house often stands a bed on four posts, raised some six feet above the floor, where young unmarried girls sleep and receive their lovers at night. During the rainy months when the cooking is necessarily done indoors, this bed is moved against the wall with the others to make room for the fires. Marital relations take place within the husband's house at dusk or at night, and pre- or extramarital relations in the women's house also at night. Frequently, however, fast and secretive intimacies occur in the daytime inside a man's house, with women of the village or with visiting Fula Kunda and Peul Fouta women who come to trade dairy products and to chat.

Within the women's house, the eldest female is said to be a leader of sorts, but her responsibilities are few. One involves keeping a supply of partly ground corn to be prepared on short notice for unexpected guests. Also, she often attends childbirth, cares for sick children, and gives advice in minor disputes. Although a system of seniority is observed by co-wives concerning morning and evening tasks, one co-wife does not have the right to punish or direct the other's behavior. Co-wives may and do borrow utensils and money, cooperate in performing numerous tasks, and address each other by their personal names. Occasionally a co-wife will sleep with the other's infants and may assist the other during childbirth. One co-wife may treat the other's illnesses, except those of the genital region. A wife never helps her husband accumulate bridewealth for another woman, but she often assists her son in this matter.

39

Tonghia consists of fifteen compounds arranged in a ring around the open village center. The circle is divided by an imaginary north-south axis into two named halves, Satian and Bantasu. Satian, the half to the east, is said by those living there to be higher, older, stronger, and more populous, and to have been the abode of the most important people in the village's history. Bantasu, they say, is "down below," the people are untrustworthy, the compounds have less sense of unity, the inhabitants are newcomers, and they tend to be inconsequential. One braggart from Satian once said, "Satian, the men; Bantasu, the women." In reality, both sides of the village were founded at the same time, Satian is on a slightly higher slope than Bantasu, and Bantasu is the more populous side. Generally, but not because of any conscious norm, the fields of Satian lie to the east of the village, and those of Bantasu to the west. The people of Bantasu refer to Satian as "up there," but deny that their half is inferior. They say, "We are two parts of the same village; we are the same thing."

Paths lead from all compounds to the village center where an enormous kapok tree grows. In the shade of this tree, toward the east lies an elevated sitting platform for the men of the village, and a smaller sitting rack is situated toward the southwest for the boys. Here the men and boys gossip, chat, and sleep away their afternoons when there is no work to be done. Here in the evening the boys and girls of the village dance, drum, wrestle, and sing. Also at the village center are three blacksmith sheds where all ironwork is done, and during the dry season there is a communal bin where peanuts are weighed and bought by the cooperative. In December 1965, the first mosque was constructed on this long-pagan communal ground.

The bipartite division of Tonghia is purely a residential phenomenon, deriving from an identical division at Timbi, the inhabitants' natal village in Guinea. No patronymic or matrisib has any more or less right on one side or the other. If a compound from Satian moved to Bantasu, it would be considered Satian for at least one generation. Two of the compounds now included in Bantasu originated on the Satian side.

Rivalry between the two sides is expressed on several occasions, the most obvious being wrestling contests held in the evening at the village center. At these events, young boys of comparable size and strength from the opposite sides are pitted against one another in a spirited match, to the rhythm of drums. The object of the contest is to cause the opponent to lose his balance and fall; young men cease wrestling once past their late teens or early twenties.

The village chief is elected by the consensus of all headmen and elders on the basis of his age and wisdom. Once elected, he holds office for life unless he proves to be incompetent. Each side of the village may retain the chieftainship as many as three successive times, whereupon the opposite side is privileged to furnish three chiefs.

Waliba, the seventh chief and a resident of Satian, is no relative of the chief who preceded him, but belongs to the same matrisib as Tonghia's founder, Waliouae. Although Waliba was not chosen through the usual elective process, he justifies his position in terms of his kinship to Waliouae. He was named chief by a Government official when the preceding chief was dismissed by the people, and was chosen on the basis of his age-tempered wisdom.

The chief of Tonghia is paid a modest sum for his labors by the Government (4,000–5,000 francs, or $16–$20) which he divides among the compounds of the village. He receives no special goods or services from people within the village, but most gifts to the village as a whole are presented to him.

The chief presides at meetings of elders, and the weight of his opinion helps decide matters when the elders espouse conflicting views. The following synopses of six village meetings suggest the range of matters brought to the elders; these meetings took place in front of the chief's house before the evening meal.

1. A Fula Kunda from the village of Sintiang Bakari reported to the game warden that a young Coniagui who resided at Tonghia had harvested palm wine from a reserved forest. When the Coniagui was fined, the elders of Tonghia decided that the entire village of Sintiang Bakari would be denied access to the services of Tonghia's

blacksmiths, upon whom the Fula Kunda depended for their tools. Waliba discovered that a blacksmith from Tonghia was selling iron tools to a Wolof man who was married to a Badyaranké woman, but who lived in the quarantined village. "If the Wolof wants tools," Waliba said, "he should first come here and publicly request pardon." Waliba then went to the guilty blacksmith and scolded him.

2. At the commencement of the rainy season, the men assembled in front of Waliba's house to discuss the price of milk. They decided that if a Fula Kunda or Peul Fouta wished to sell milk at Tonghia, the price would be two cups for five francs (two cents). Another matter they decided was that all sheep and goats be tethered so that they would not damage the new crops. Any animal found in a field would become the property of the landowner until the animal's owner made restitution for crop losses. Or the field's owner, if he preferred, could kill the animal outright.

3. A girl from the Badyaranké village of Patin Kouta left her family and fiancé to join her lover at Tonghia. The chief of Patin Kouta sent a delegation of elders to Tonghia to ask for the girl's return. Waliba decided that the girl should return to her father, but if she ran away again, the Tonghia people would not be responsible.

4. Someone had made a mysterious sacrifice of a chicken, salt, and charcoal at the village center, and some villagers became alarmed because the village center is a critical area and sorcery done there would affect everyone. A meeting was called to determine the explanation for the sacrifice. Before the elders had congregated, a young man confessed that a marabout had recommended that particular sacrifice to him so that his mistress, who was about to marry another man, would return to him. But this young man had once been accused of attempting to "eat the soul" of an elder by witchcraft, so the elders decided to meet and discuss the matter at length. They determined that the sacrificer's purpose was not to harm the villagers, but that in the future, a person should notify his father or headman in advance before making private sacrifices at the village center. The discussion

then changed to the subject of a family of Peul Fouta that was coming to live with one of the headmen for the duration of the growing season.

5. The elders gathered to decide, as they do every year, that Friday should be a day of rest during the growing season. Anyone caught working on Friday would have to forfeit a gourdful of honey beer. Secondly, they discussed complaints that cows from the Peul Fouta village of Koel had wandered through some Badyaranké fields. Waliba sent a young man from his compound to ask the Koel chief "if the Government gave him permission to graze his cows on our fields."

6. A man from Tonghia had cleared a peanut field near the Peul Fouta village of Koel. The Koel people asked him to abandon the field and move elsewhere because their cows would certainly endanger his crops. The Badyaranké owner said that he could not clear a new field by himself before planting time, so the Peul Fouta agreed to provide a work party of young men to help him clear land where their cattle would be less likely to cause damage (for which they would be held responsible). Consequently, the man did not sow his first field, but the people of Koel never fulfilled their promise. Eventually it became too late to plant peanuts that year, and the man lost his entire cash crop. The men of Tonghia assembled and planted millet in the original field; they told the chief of Koel that should the millet be destroyed, Koel inhabitants would be expected to compensate the owner in cash.

Meetings of the elders are invariably called in anticipation of the arrival of medical immunization teams or officials from the agricultural cooperative (the Government's purchasing agency for the peanut crop), and for the announcement of any directives or information from the office of the *chef d'Arrondissement* at Bonconto. No cases of fighting or adultery were brought before the elders during my stay in the village; these matters, when they are resolved at all, are settled at the individual or compound level. In pre-French times, accusations of homicide were cleared before a Badyaranké chief and elders, and the "convicted" killer's

Top, *a meeting of the village elders;* bottom, *the Koranic school in session at Tonghia.*

44

matrisib was given the responsibility for his execution. This kind of situation has never happened at Tonghia, and no one there knows of any such incidents elsewhere. Elders also intervene in cases where a villager neglects to participate in collective labors, such as the clearing of fire lanes or road repair, by fining him. If he should continue to be recalcitrant, the elders would forbid anyone to work in his fields. I learned of no instance in which this sanction was necessary, and such extreme uncooperativeness is rare.

WORK GROUPS

Boys from approximately nine to twenty years of age, of whom there are some thirty in Tonghia, belong to a work society known as the *patumbare*. Equal in number to the boys, the young men twenty to thirty-five years old are members of another society, the palau. Each group elects a leader who acts as treasurer; the society can be contracted by anyone in the village for a half or full day's work, and the treasurer handles the arrangements. Leaders of the two societies are elected from among the eldest of their members. Once elected, they serve for three years; leadership is supposed to alternate between Satian and Bantasu. Payment for the group's work is made to the leader at the end of the harvest in cash when the villagers' money has been replenished from their peanut sales. Previously, the men of the palau were paid in cash, grain, or animals, the last two to be consumed after the harvest by the entire village at a great feast. For the last two years the intention has been to accumulate a pool of cash from which members of the respective societies might borrow for bridewealth payments, taxes, or unexpected expenses. Both societies charge 1,500 francs ($6) for a half day's labor and 2,500 francs ($10) for a full day, with rate reductions for members. In 1965, all fields worked by the two societies belonged to private individuals, whereas in the past they labored on collective fields (marouba). Not infrequently these societies are asked to work fields belonging to other villages and other ethnic groups.

The young unmarried girls of the village organize from time to time under the eldest of their group, who acts as foreman and treasurer. The girls demand 150 francs (60 cents) apiece for a full day's hoeing, and with this money they provide a feast for the entire village. In all cases, the field owner provides food, water, tobacco, and kola nuts for the workers.

The simplest way to attract workers is to announce that on a certain day there will be honey beer or cooked meat available for all who come to help. If the incentive is beer, such an event is called a *wampanyi*; if there is much meat, it is a *babaré*; and if the owner offers only a goat or a couple of chickens, it is a *kilé*. Less frequent than these is the "in-law" work (*bitondoku*) — a group assembled by a young man to help in his prospective father-in-law's fields. Women work their rice plots individually, but occasionally they combine efforts into an informal group known as a *wandubé*. Then they collectively work the participants' plots; the "hostesses" are required to feed the workers. However, no money ever circulates in the labor exchanges between women.

### THE YEARLY CYCLE

The year is divided into two seasons, *partio* and *wonké*. Partio begins in June with the rainy period and sowing, and terminates in August well before the end of the rains when the first crops are harvested. Wonké — from August to May — includes the harvests, the end of the rains, and the entire dry season. The early weeks of partio are known as *cumpasse*, the time of planting. The remainder of partio after cumpasse is the season for hoeing and weeding. Wonké begins with *codr*, the time of harvest; during this period the rains end, and the peanuts, corn, rice, millet, and cotton crops are gathered. The coldest part of the year coincides with that subdivision of codr known as *sandiana*, when the women cut rice by day and the village is quiet, dark, and cold at night. At the termination of codr, the days become progressively hotter as wonké continues.

After the heaviest work of harvesting has been completed, many young men leave the village to do wage labor. (In 1965, twenty young men from Tonghia left for this purpose, mostly in groups of three with occasional comrades from other villages and other tribes.) They travel by truck to the city of Thiés where they harvest peanuts for Wolof landowners, for wages lower than more acculturated locals would accept. With these earnings they buy manufactured clothing for themselves and others at Tonghia, bicycles, radios, watches, and numerous minor paraphernalia such as combs, mirrors, perfumes, amulets, and photographs of themselves with their companions. The young men leave during sandiana; while they are away, there is no singing or dancing at the village center. This is also the time when the old people huddle around fires in their houses during the cold nights, and many take sick. The strong young men are far away, everyone is tired from several months of sustained hard work, and the villagers feel unprotected and weak.

The period from January, after the return of the young men from Thiés, until the next rains is one of relative leisure. At this time, villagers travel, perhaps to Velingara to lounge around the town, to Guinea to visit relatives, to Gambia to buy imported goods, or to Portuguese Guinea to stock up on five-gallon bottles of gin. Peddlers, musicians, and strangers to the area invade the countryside. The Fula Kunda and Peul Fouta come to graze their cattle in the now empty rice fields, since the grass in the forest where they normally feed has turned dry and brittle. By the time the rains arrive, the new clothes are worn through, the radios and wristwatches broken, and the bicycles often sold. The rains bring everyone back to his own village, travel and travellers decrease, and the traditional white and indigo native cotton clothing again becomes the common garb. The ring of the blacksmith's hammer is heard as he prepares new tools, and the work cycle begins again.

## RELATIONS WITH THE FULA KUNDA AND THE PEUL FOUTA

Traditional Badyaranké society recognized no political authority more inclusive than the village chief. Never, even during the wars with the seminomadic cattle people (the Fula Kunda and Peul Fouta) at the end of the last century, did the Badyaranké complement their strong sense of cultural identity with one of political unity. To my knowledge, the only recurrent intervillage activity is the yearly fishing expedition. In Guinea, most of the Bad-yaranké villages and many Fula Kunda and Peul Fouta organize in order to trap fish in one of the deep tributaries of the Kayanga River. In Senegal, the villages of Paroumba, Patin Kouta, Tonghia, Dialiadian, Sare Oura, and numerous smaller villages of Fula Kunda and Peul Fouta cooperate during one day in the spring to trap fish in a nearby stream.

Before the fishing begins, some elders make an offering of cooked food to the water, "so that the crocodile will keep his jaws closed that day." The people of Tonghia say that they are reluctant to participate in this communal fishing expedition because the elders of Paroumba are the ones who address the crocodile; the Tonghia people suspect that the elders of Paroumba give the crocodile permission to bite people of other villages in exchange for sparing their own. This rite to close the mouth of the crocodile is the most inclusive activity of a religious nature practiced by the traditional Badyaranké.

Another relation with peoples outside the village involves cattle. Many Badyaranké own a few cows which they consign to the nomads. The milk products and often a calf from each cow are kept by the herder as payment. Cattle serve primarily as bride-wealth payments, and the nomads act as a kind of bank, holding the beasts in trust until required. At the village of Patin Kouta, however, some Badyaranké have begun to care for their own herds. The practice of entrusting cattle to the nomads may soon disappear; the Government agricultural cooperative has recently introduced small plows which, through use of animal power, make it possible to extend the areas of cultivation. For this reason, some Tonghia residents have already found it more convenient to keep their cattle at home.

Often Fula Kunda or Peul Fouta contract the young men's work societies (palau and patumbare) to work their fields in exchange for a cow or cash. On one occasion the entire male population of Tonghia helped a few families of Fula Kunda clear forest and brush so that they could found a new village.

Despite these numerous channels of cooperation, the Badyaranké dislike the nomads. They claim that the cattle herders are transient, whereas they themselves are sedentary; they believe the cattle herders to be ultimately unreliable, avaricious, and spiteful. Although the Badyaranké men may have intercourse with visiting Fula Kunda and Peul Fouta women, intermarriage is rare. Most Badyaranké do have close friends among these other tribes, but in theory it is not considered good to have such friends.

Islam is providing a rapprochement between the younger generations of the neighboring tribes that clearly erodes the traditional tribal notions of integrity. The older generations of pagan Badyaranké and Fula Kunda have more in common with each other than with the generations soon to replace them, and they look more and more toward each other for companionship, especially when there is some beer or palm wine to be drunk.

## CHAPTER THREE

*External*
*Powers*

A boy works in his father's fields as soon as he is old enough to sling stones at a foraging crow or monkey. For the remainder of his years he courts the hard soil until he no longer has the strength to labor with his tools under the strong sun. Men and women work industriously to assure that their granaries will contain enough to eat from one harvest until the next. The Badyaranké are proud of their reputation for being diligent cultivators, and their achievements with simple hand implements are praiseworthy. A strong back and willingness to work are essential to the man who wishes to eat, acquire wives, and support children. But work alone is not sufficient, for harmony must be sought with a variety of invisible forces if the products of his sweat are to reach fruition.

Although the powers described in this chapter differ in many respects, all are external [1] to man. Some, such as the shrines and bow and arrow sorcery may be controlled through human initiative; others, which include the evil breezes and certain dangerous animals, cannot be manipulated or otherwise harnessed for deliberate ends. The powers also differ in the degrees to which humans may be held blamefully responsible for their effects. A mother believed to have killed her child by sorcery would be disdained and probably punished; whereas a mother who lost her child because she ignored the postpartum sex taboo would only be considered intemperate. The powers may also be viewed according to whether they influence individual or collective welfare. The supreme deity (Kodan) may devastate an entire village, or even the whole countryside if he chooses to do so, but the timid forest sprites engage only in direct contracts with selected individuals.

## VILLAGE AND COMPOUND RITES

According to the story about the arrival of the first Badyaranké at Tonghia, a Manding marabout [2] conferred with some local genies (dyinné) to learn if they would permit a village to be built. (The Badyaranké believe that genies are the most powerful of God's creations; not all mortals are said to have the ability to see them, but genies are supposed to resemble men, except for their light color, feline eyes, pointed noses, white hair, and long beards. A tornado whirled from the east and stirred up leaves, indicating to the marabout that the eastern genies were favorably disposed, but that those of the west were not. He said that the eastern

[1] This distinction in spiritual powers was suggested to me by the following passage from Mary Douglas's important work dealing with religious pollution *Purity and Danger:* "The spiritual powers which human action can unleash can roughly be divided into two classes — internal and external. The first reside within the psyche of the agent — such as the evil eye, witchcraft, gifts of vision or prophecy. The second are external symbols on which the agent must consciously work: spells, blessings, curses, charms and formulas and invocations. These powers require actions by which spiritual power is discharged" (1966:98).
[2] A marabout, to the Badyaranké, refers to anyone who is slightly conversant with the Koran, or with written Arabic. By virtue of their learning, such individuals are considered to be the most powerful magical technicians. Their role as religious leader, diviner, and curer has been described by Vincent Monteil in his *L'Islam Noir.*

genies persuaded their western neighbors to allow the Badyaranké to settle, and the village was established despite an ambiguous mandate.

The marabout then attached an amulet containing a Koranic verse to each end of a wooden pestle; he instructed two young men to hold the pestle and allow themselves to be directed by its will. They were drawn to a tree (of the species *Daniella oliveri*) where genies were said to reside. The chief of the new village, Waliouae, hid an axe and told the marabout that if he uncovered it, they would believe his divination. The marabout placed the pestle on the boys' shoulders and directed them to find the axe. They ran to where the axe was hidden and the marabout said, "If it is not there, go on." But the pestle did not direct the young men to move, and the people knew the marabout's words were authentic. He told them that a "red" goat was to be sacrificed and eaten at the base of this tree every third year before the arrival of the rains, and that the genies in turn would protect the villagers, guide them toward their sundry needs, and permit their seeds to grow and ripen.

Every three years, with one memorable exception, the men and older boys, led by the village chief, have performed the sacrifice and shared in the feast. The rite was once neglected for more than three years, and the "slighted" genies were believed to have burned the entire village. A fire began on the eastern, or Satian, side of the village, and there its effects were most ravaging. The Satian people believe they were hardest hit because they are more important and thus more responsible to the genies.

According to a current version of village history, the marabout found a passage in his Koran revealing that a female genie with many children lives near a tree on the western side of Tonghia. Here the women, led by the eldest among them, consecrate rice paste collected from every compound to the virulent genies, who are thought to assure the women's health and fertility. As the oblation is placed in winnowing baskets at the foot of the tree, the women make their requests. In June 1965 they said:

Chief's wife no. 1: I do this for the village, for the planting, so the rice will push well, so there will be many children here, and not too many bad things.

Chief's wife no. 2: May God give us a good rainy season with no sickness in the village and not too much witchcraft.

Third woman: The *cowaeo* [an owl thought to be a Fula Kunda witch] cried last night. May the witches who are in debt kill not other people's children, but their own.

Fourth woman: May my rice grow well, and my children have no sickness.

This rite is performed one week after the men's sacrifice, every third year. Although no males or pregnant women may participate, a woman who fears a difficult childbirth may ease her labor by lying near the tree. Pregnant women avoid the rite because they believe that rice paste, when eaten, could harm a male fetus.

Both men's and women's sacrifices are addressed to genies, but are also said to be heeded by Kodan himself who lives at a great remove in the heavens. The Badyaranké believe that although neither Kodan nor the genies can be obligated, bought, or otherwise controlled by human actions, they are normally benevolent if their simple, recurrent demands are satisfied. Chief Waliba, who is less impressed than most Badyaranké about the credibility of marabout divinations, maintains that the sacrificial sites were disclosed in a dream, perhaps to a seer (*umadisé*) who communicated directly with the genies.

Each year, after the harvests have been collected and the young men have returned from their labors in the north of Senegal, a village communal feast of thanksgiving takes place, called the offering (sada) of the hundred plates. This feast consists of a redistribution of cooked food from all compounds, held at the village center. The entire population participates, male and female, old and young. The men eat together on their sitting platform, and the women eat apart, seated on the ground. The chief and elders speak to Kodan, the genies, and the dead to thank them for the harvest, to ask them to protect the village from fire, and to ensure continued well-being. The people of Tonghia say that this rite was borrowed from the Islamized Manding.

The preceding sacrifices and the feast of the hundred plates are performed at regular intervals. However, occasional sacrifices

53

involving the entire village are invariably prescribed by a marabout in the event of some unexpected and threatening situation. On one such occasion a young man learned from a marabout that someone in the village was about to "eat" (by witchcraft) the soul of another person, and by virtue of the culprit's anonymity, the situation became a public danger. The marabout prescribed that the men of the village should redistribute kola nuts among themselves to ward off the imminent attack. On another occasion a Manding passing through Tonghia on his bicycle said that a marabout in his village had predicted there would be inadequate rain for the growing season together with an invasion of locusts, and had advised a redistribution. In the evening, Waliba assembled the elders in his compound; they decided to carry out this prescription themselves at the village center. On the appointed day, most of the adult males gathered by the sitting platform with a handful of kola nuts, or a gourd of shelled peanuts, or a lump of millet paste. Waliba asked that the rains would come and that the crops would not be eaten by locusts. The blacksmiths then passed the three elements — kola nuts, peanuts, and paste — around to the participants. This ceremony was addressed to Kodan, and its form, like the regular village sacrifice, was a simple, non-contractual request. Natural disasters like drought and locusts are not conceived of as punishment for human omission or error, and no one is blamed if such a mishap occurs.

The men of an individual compound may offer a ladle of palm wine or honey beer to a stone representing the deceased father of their headman. When this rite was performed in my compound, Waliba took the stone from its resting place under his bed and placed it to the right of his doorstep. Such offerings to a compound's ancestor occur in late May or early June when the dark heavy clouds begin to cluster and rumble; at this time, the headman beseeches the ancestor to favor the compound's dependents with sound bodies and full stomachs. Although formerly practiced by all headmen and any other adult males who wished to, the rite has been abandoned by all Moslems and many non-Moslems. Only three men at Tonghia continue to honor their fathers in this fashion.

A Badyaranké addresses his father in his role as a provider and never should promise repayment if the harvest is indeed successful. A person could never request the father to remove illness or to send injury to someone. The ancestral stone itself should be passed down from father to son, but I know of one young man who took the abandoned stone of his mother's brother, which thereafter became the young man's father.

The traditional alcoholic libation to an individual's father has been replaced by an Islamic Manding rite which is performed by pagan and Moslem alike at the moment when the fields come back to life. The oblation consists of lumps of millet paste, placed in a winnowing basket at the base of the post in the compound's center. The headman squats by the basket with the other men of his compound and each addresses Kodan directly. With palms turned upward, they ask for "protection during the rainy season, courage to work in the fields, not much sickness in the compound, a good harvest, and Kodan's protection of the fields from wild animals." The paste is then given for all to eat, including women and children of the compound. When the paste is eaten, the children shout, "Sadao!" (literally "alms"), because "God likes to hear the cries of little children." This shout terminates the sacrifice. In every compound after the first maize has been collected, a paste is prepared by the women and placed by the post at the compound center. The men thank Kodan for the crops, ask protection for the harvest and the granaries, and request that he allow people to eat in good health. All the residents consume the paste as before and the children's shouts end the rite. The Badyaranké say that if the people of a compound neglect this sacrifice they will have less grain than those who remember to do it.

THE MARABOUT

Islamic elements have been incorporated into Badyaranké magical practices far longer than any Tonghia resident has been a Moslem. Three basic types of prescription, which cover a vast range of problems, can be purchased from the marabouts. These are the Koranic amulets (*kahiti*), Koranic waters (*nassi*), and sada.

The Koranic amulets, widely known in Senegal as gris-gris, are

Top, *a funeral sacrifice being performed in a compound;* bottom, *a hunter with many amulets.*

made in profuse shapes and materials; they are said to provide their owner with assurance against a multitude of anxieties. The gris-gris are commonly worn around the biceps, wrist, or waist, and usually consist of a leather packet with a message sewn inside. Some are meant to confer virility, courage, intelligence, wisdom, prosperity, and popularity; others to protect the wearer against injury; still others to allow a person to control another's thoughts. The following list includes most of the written amulets known to the Badyaranké together with their reputed powers.

| | |
|---|---|
| *baladan* | Worn by men, this is made of cloth and leather and can be worn anywhere on the person, and is often suspended over the inside of the owner's doorway. The message is always wrapped in crocodile skin; it protects against iron, but not against silver or gold. |
| *balakantaran* | This class includes all amulets whose papers contain words that protect the wearer's body from external danger of any kind. |
| *bamburan* | These charms are used by male wrestlers only, and strapped to the front and back of their chests. If a person should travel at night and encounter dangerous animals, the amulets make them hide on his approach and avoid him. |
| *boindiran* | This amulet makes the owner's adversary fall, and is often worn by a wrestler. It can be carried anywhere on the body, and is usually worn by men. |
| *bouloudoun* | This is the name for a general class of amulets worn on the forearm or wrist to help the owners avoid fear. Also, a person will be unable to refuse the wearer's request to borrow money. These are worn by men, and cost approximately 200 francs (80 cents). |
| *daridyaran* | When a person wants to be liked by everyone, he wraps the daridyaran paper along with a certain leaf, perfume, and earth from the village center, a market, and the doorway of a mosque. The amulets can be worn anywhere on the body, and by both men and women. |
| *dibi dibi* | These amulets are worn on the forearm and wrist and make the owner invisible so that he can steal another person's wife or whatever else he desires. The charm is often made of the skin of a black cat, or of leather painted black, and the message about the desired object is written at midnight when everyone is asleep. |

| | |
|---|---|
| *katume* | This type includes any amulet containing a paper with someone's name written on it. If, for example, a person wants the elders of the village to elect him to public office, he writes their names on the paper. If he suspects a certain person is committing adultery with his wife, or is stealing from his house, the owner writes the other's name on the paper in order to catch him. Also, an individual can write the names of two people to make them quarrel, or of a person to make him go mad. Ordinarily a katume is worn, but if many names are contained in it, it is buried at the village center. To make two people argue, the owner must add hot peppers and dog excrement and bury the katume where the women throw trash. This charm can also be hung over the doorway to prevent a particular witch from entering the house. |
| *mankané* | Worn or carried in the pocket, the charm protects against someone who wants to hit the wearer; the attacker falls down and cannot get up. The wearer adds seven scorpion stingers, seven hot peppers, seven red ants, and the excrement of a donkey to the packet. |
| *matyana* or *kabala* | Suspended over the shoulder to hang on the side, this charm can be worn by men or women, but more often by women to help ease pregnancy ills and aches in the ribs. It can protect against metal, knives, and witches. |
| *nambo* | If the wearer wants to become important, no one can prevent him. This amulet is worn around the waist and is fastened in front. |
| *nembali* | If an individual has this amulet, no one will accuse him of being a liar because the accuser will die within five days. The paper is placed in a goat's horn and carried in the pocket, or worn around the neck or upper arm. |
| *orto* | To make this death-dealing amulet, the owner writes a victim's name on a paper, sews it in a leather packet, and attaches it to the tip of a sickle. If this cuts a living plant, the individual whose name is within will die. The marabout, leather worker, and blacksmith, who made the paper, packet, and sickle, respectively, are forbidden to speak to anyone until the plant is cut. As an alternative method, the purchaser may bury the packet in a grave. The cost is 500 francs ($2). |

| | |
|---|---|
| *patyutyana* | This is a message sewn on a twig that the owner uses to scrape his teeth clean with. All that he says is believed true, and is applauded even if it consists of lies. Patyutyana is used by men, specifically by the village chief. |
| *pudike* | This word refers to any amulet made with a goat's horn, which can be worn on the arm or around the waist and used by either men or women. The charm's powers vary, depending on what is written on the paper inside. Most often a man places the amulet under his bed so that his woman will not be unfaithful. |
| *safé kanafa* | This consists of a packet sewn on the hat of a person who wants to become important, feared, and respected. The paper is enclosed within a piece of lion skin. |
| *sisila* | This amulet is worn around the neck by men or women, and in general serves to protect the body. |
| *sitikun* | These charms are used by robbers. The bearer can ask for the key to a person's trunk and receive it. The robber takes what he wants and the victim cannot wake up until he leaves. This amulet can be put under a stone, or placed in an animal horn to be carried in the pocket. It may contain the tail of a hyena, and is used only by men. |
| *sunkutukedyow* | If a person carries this amulet, he becomes very likable. If he is a peddler, everyone will buy his wares. It can be worn like a sisila or as a wolo wolo. |
| *tamadan* | Women wear this amulet on their heads. The tamadan may contain written papers but often serves as decoration only. |
| *tuso* | A special amulet worn on the upper arm, this protects the owner against being accused of petty mischief; if he has done something that merits a prison sentence, the authorities will never realize it. Also it protects against snake bite. |
| *wolo wolo* | Worn on the upper arm by both men and women, this amulet makes everyone who sees the wearer like him, and protects him against those with evil intentions. |

Koranic waters (nassi) are prescribed and sold for many of the same situations as the written amulets, and similarly, they are generally intended for individual use. The client explains his needs to the marabout, who selects an appropriate sentence from the Koran, which he writes in washable ink on a wooden tablet. He then spills water over the tablet and collects the sentence, now in solution, in a bottle. The client then pays the marabout; if the marabout lives in the same village or is a personal acquaintance, the client pays when and if his needs have been realized.

Koranic waters divide into two major types which can be described as positive and negative. Positive waters make one prosperous, protect against dangers such as witchcraft, sorcery, or weapons, promise success on a trip, and make one attractive to the opposite sex. The user pours the liquid into his hands and applies it to his skin, rubbing from the extremities toward the trunk, to absorb the power of the water. Some waters may be drunk, specifically to poison the user's body so that if a witch attempts to eat his soul, the witch himself will die.

Negative waters, on the other hand, are supposed to remove something believed to be lodged inside the body, such as bad fortune, an unwelcome genie, or magical poison. The user rubs the negative waters on his skin in the direction from the trunk toward the extremities, to remove the problem.

Usually a bottle of Koranic water is buried under the doorway of a newly constructed house, or under the central post of a new compound. In both cases it protects the family and ensures good fortune. These liquids may cost as little as 10 francs (4 cents) or more than 1,000 francs ($4) depending on the reputation of the particular marabout and the solvency of the client.

When the young men of Tonghia leave to labor for wages in the north of Senegal, they consult marabouts for advice on what sada they should make for a safe journey. During my stay, the offerings made included trailing cotton behind the men as they left the village, and arranging little piles of kola nuts or cotton thread where two paths converged. To ensure their safe return, a marabout instructed the children of these men to eat a mixture of milk, sugar, and rice. Marabouts also advised other kinds of sada. One man was told to wear a copper bracelet to protect his body from witches. Another wore a silver ring in expectation of wealth. A third man was advised to release a spotted chicken in his compound so that his children's good health might continue. A young student in Dakar who wished to pass an examination which would enable him to study in France was instructed by a marabout to release a white chicken in his home compound which should never be eaten. Because the student was far from home, he wrote to a kinsman at Tonghia (I translated the letter) who carried out the instructions. Such offerings are extremely common and account for numerous oddities at forks in the path, animals that are not eaten, and most of the rings, bracelets, and necklaces worn.

An individual who feels that he has been cheated, threatened, or humiliated may request a marabout to prescribe an amulet or formulate a spell that will injure the supposed malefactor. Such deliberately harmful procedures are recognized as a separate category of action by the Badyaranké, and are herein referred to as sorcery, following an earlier usage by E. E. Evans-Pritchard.[3] The most dreaded of techniques known to marabouts is the bow and arrow sorcery (*korté*). The marabout utters a spell and performs a variety of symbolic actions, such as piercing an egg with a needle, by which an "arrow" is released which is said to carry injury or death to its victim. The "arrow" may even be sent to destroy someone's field, and various charms or twig constructions are often seen at the point where a path enters a field, and are put there to stop the arrow's flight. If the victim is sufficiently prepared, or has been forewarned, he may divert the "arrow," which must then return to pique its sender. A Badyaranké from Tonghia, who had acquired a reputation for sexual exploits with other men's wives, suffered a disease (perhaps polio) which withered one of his legs. All of his acquaintances assume that an anonymous cuckold successfully propelled an "arrow" into this adulterer's leg, and thereby balanced his excesses. A marabout is apparently without moral responsibility when he assists in such enterprises, and whether or not his clients are justified depends on one's point of view. The man with the withered leg, for example, considered his misfortune to be undeserved.

Marabouts say that the Koran knows whether a specific problem

3 1937:8–9.

demands an offering, a Koranic amulet, or a Koranic water. All may serve collective interests (for example, an amulet or liquid bought by a chief for the entire village), but situations involving collectivities are generally served by the sada. All three categories can be used for individual ends, but the sada is most often used in response to a crisis, whereas amulets and waters act as long-term safeguards. All are used by pagans and Moslems, and may be bought by anyone from any marabout. Use of these medicines is public, expected, and universal. No one envies another for purchasing a medicine that will improve his lot because they are available to all. Even the most self-assured Badyaranké requires a collection of amulets and liquids. Waliba, because of his role as village chief, owns an amulet with which he scrapes his teeth every Friday morning to assure that his words will be true, wise, and applauded.

Although most amulets and spells are prescribed by marabouts, some are purely pagan in origin. Such amulets (*tafu*) resemble those made by a marabout, but rather than written messages, they "contain" secret verses; these are recited into a cotton cord, which is knotted and worn around the arm, neck, or waist, or is sometimes hung over the door. Tafu protect against snakes, scorpions, crocodiles, and witches, and may expedite sexual or material desires. Their power derives from the recited spell, which may be learned by anyone, pagan and Moslem alike.

One Tonghia elder told me about a spell (*cobanyi*) that protects vegetables and fruits from light-fingered passersby. The pilferer upon eating his spoils will suffer a magical sickness which is curable only by the one who cast the spell. Instructions for casting spells are occasionally sold, and the elder mentioned above offered to impart his technique to me for the Senegalese equivalent of eighty cents, the price he had paid to learn it.

THE CONTRACTUAL SHRINE

An invisible, powerful force called *koasé* (translated as "shrine") is said to inhabit certain stones found usually near tree roots. The individual to whom the force is supposed to have revealed itself becomes its custodian, and his permission should be sought

62

by anyone who wishes to request the shrine's services. Anything may be asked of the shrine, but it must always be in terms of an equitable contract. A man might, for example, promise to pay the shrine a chicken for a safe journey; or he might promise a cow in exchange for the death of a hated enemy. If the request is granted and the client welshes, the Badyaranké believe that the force will leave its abode in the stone, may first turn into a wind and blow around the debtor's house to warn him, and if payment is still withheld, may injure or even kill its recalcitrant client.

The force within the shrine is said to be mysterious, but to be visible to seers, and occasionally to visit the village as an animal or a whirlwind. Tonghia people speak of three specialized shrines in Guinea which offer success in fishing, war, and hunting. These powerful shrines are said to be seldom visited, for they require human lives in payment. One legend states that the Badyaranké once offered the shrine permission to take the lives of certain Fula Kunda in exchange for allowing the Badyaranké a bountiful catch of fish. A Badyaranké, not a Fula Kunda, was bitten by a crocodile during the fishing, however, thus indicating to the people that Badyaranké stomachs may only be filled through the exchange of Badyaranké lives. A similar price, demanded by the shrine for military victory, was reported to be the lives of the bravest warriors, who would die in the front lines of battle or shortly thereafter.

At the village of Wankan in Guinea is a shrine that once was visited by hunters desirous of good fortune. The story is told that the chief of Wankan, realizing this was a powerful shrine, decided to acquire it for the entire village. Hunters paid the shrine with meat, but the chief offered to give it the lives of two of the best people in the community if it would serve them all. That is why this shrine is now known as "two mouths," for it requires two human lives in order to grant good luck. Sometimes a whirlwind was seen leaving the shrine, which was supposed to be the koasé itself going to the river to drink; to pacify the koasé, the women would tap gourd bowls and it would return. Today this shrine still exists, but the village itself has been aban-

63

doned because many inhabitants became blind. A mystical smoke is thought to linger there — which resembles the "heat" of women, was perhaps sent by genies, and is damaging to the eyes.

Another shrine is said to grant life rather than demand it: at the village of Temanto in Senegal is a tree where barren women come to ask for children. Their request is expressed as follows: "I have come. I have no children, and I have come to you to ask you to give me a child. When I have a child, I will return to pay you with millet beer." Still another shrine, owned by an old Fula Kunda woman, is said to require human lives, regardless of whether the request is large or small.

Badyaranké often consult shrines which are owned — in their territory or near their villages — by the Manding and Fula Kunda, and I visited one that belongs to a wizened old Fula Kunda hunter at the village of Akan. The following account was compiled from the hunter's words.

The shrine is older than the hunter and his village. It was handed down from his grandfather. It consists of a stone at the foot of a tree; he does not know how it was found nor what force dwells there. However, if not used from time to time, the force will depart. If someone wants to approach the shrine, he asks the hunter's permission, but goes there alone. If the hunter (owner) went, he would be responsible if the guest did not pay as he promised. If a person's son has been killed by a witch, that person can ask that the witch be given a certain, recognizable sickness within two days. If the petitioner sees someone with that sickness, he pays whatever was promised — a goat, chicken, etc. — and eats the sacrificed animal by the shrine, never in the village; a portion of the meat is given to the stone. A witch cannot eat at the shrine because he knows it will be harmful to him. A petitioner cannot wear black clothes, only white. Among the requests that the shrine grants are: killing a witch after he has been identified; harming someone who stole from the petitioner; enabling a wife to have children. Also, a child may be taken there and entrusted to the shrine, to mature under its protection; if the child grows up safely, the parent pays the promised fee.

The Tonghia people say that this particular shrine has lost some of its power. Several years ago a Fula Kunda paid the shrine a bull in fulfillment of his promise, but erred by taking the skin back to the village to sell. Soon afterwards the man died. It is thought the shrine's power ran out, and that it may now even lie and deceive, though it still has the force to do harm.

There are at least two other important variants of the contractual shrine: the nightjar shrine (*koasé fédé*) and the caterpillar shrine (*koasé kuntuntar*), which will be described in more detail below.

When a marabout prescribes a sada, it may resemble the sacrifices made to the pagan shrines. Indeed, the Badyaranké often use the term koasé to describe any rite where a libation or oblation is made or an animal destroyed. The distinctions between the traditional shrines and the offerings are not clear, but the following paragraph attempts to clarify their meanings.

A shrine exists in nature and can be discovered, whereas an offering is in most cases recommended by a marabout. The village sacrificial rites fall between these two, for they take place at the locations where genies dwell, spirits to whom marabouts prescribe offerings. Thus it is no accident that Waliba, the elder chief, refers to such rites as koasé, while the younger Moslems refer to them as sada. An offering may involve blood sacrifice, a redistribution of kola nuts, a libation of water on the lintel of a house, or simply the wearing of a copper bracelet. But the element of conditional contract, generally associated with commerce with the shrines, is less explicit in the offering. One pagan informant told me: "The sada is a salute to God. It is a message sent to God, as in the assuring of good passage for one who is dead. A shrine is a thing of the ground."

## SACRIFICE BY THE MATRISIB

Although the matrisib may assemble with other relatives and friends for a funeral ceremony, only in one particular sacrifice known as the padunko does the matrisib alone participate. Performed exclusively by the matrisib, the rite is the sole occasion when members assemble to the exclusion of outsiders. In fact, the effective group includes only the matrisib relatives of the particular village where the rite transpires. The matrisib sacrifice (padunko) is a variant of shrine (koasé) because it involves a conditional request, and if the request is granted, payment is made according to what was promised.

The sacrifice of the matrisib is essentially piacular and is performed only in times of trouble. The last padunko at Tonghia was held two years before my arrival in 1964, but I was able to collect notes on nine occurrences. The rite was performed for the following persons: a pregnant woman who had lost two previous children and feared losing a third; an infant boy with a cold; a young man to prevent his being conscripted into the French army (performed twice with successful results); a pregnant woman who had difficulty giving birth; a woman with stomach troubles; a childless woman who wanted children; a young girl as protection since she was about to be excised; and a woman with a running tropical sore.

In seven cases, the rite was initiated by a mother in behalf of her child, and twice by women for themselves. The usual procedure leading up to the rite is outlined in the following example. First, the mother goes to the oldest woman of her sib in the village to ask her to perform the rite for her child. The older woman finds a stone and places it at the head of her bed inside the women's house. Since the senior woman of a compound generally sleeps to the right of the front door, the rite is generally performed just inside the door, to the right. In the morning before eating, the senior woman brings a calabash full of water and addresses the stone as if it were her mother and grandmother. She promises to pay a cock and a hen of any color at a later date, if the mother's request is realized. Then she washes the stone with half the water, and she, the mother, and the child drink the remaining half. This example is the ideal pattern, but there can be variations. One young expectant mother had no elder female relative in the village, so she requested her husband's mother to perform the rite for her. On one occasion a padunko was done for a girl by her father's sister, while on another, a woman directly addressed the stone as her deceased mother, her mother's mother, and also her father.

The Badyaranké have no elaborate beliefs about ghosts and

66

ancestors, and they are not even certain that the dead matrilineal ancestors addressed in the sacrifice can actually send misfortune to living people. But the Badyaranké do think it is possible for ancestors to alleviate misfortune. In a padunko, they are simply trying to tempt the sacrificer's deceased mother and grandmother to help if they want to, and if they can. A person could never invoke these ancestors to do another injury or to make a positive contribution to his own welfare.

If a request is granted (the difficulty having been overcome), all the matrisib relatives of the petitioning mother assemble in the late afternoon in the compound where the contract was made. The cock and hen, provided by the mother, are killed by a male of the matrisib, and all join in a commemorative meal. The villagers say that this food causes illness if eaten by someone not in the matrisib, but there are exceptions: one mother brought some of the sacrificial meal to an old man who belonged to her father's matrisib, and another woman gave some of the food to her son's child. If the request is never realized, no payments are made and no communal meal occurs. (On one occasion, however, a mother was advised by a marabout to pay first in order to receive what she had requested.) If the request is realized and the person neglects to pay, the illness or hardship is supposed to return.

A Badyaranké woman sacrifices to her dead mother when under duress, just as she turns to her living mother for comfort when misfortune threatens or during a convalescence. The contractual form of a sacrificial request has no analogy, to my knowledge, in social relations with a living mother.

MYSTICAL CONTAMINATION

Healthy young women and small children are considered especially vulnerable to sicknesses that are believed to emanate from a variety of forest creatures, of which the long-tailed nightjar is supposed to be the most deadly. This little bird flies and sings during the dim hours of early morning and evening, and builds its nest on the ground. Badyaranké think that if a mother, her child, or even its father touch the nest, eggs, feathers, or particularly the bird itself, the child will be in critical danger. Because of this, a woman who loses several children might suspect that she had touched the bird unwittingly or at a forgotten time in the past, and make a sacrifice as a precautionary measure against further deaths.

An elderly man at Tonghia inherited a fieldstone from his father which, it is said, could be used to cleanse parents worried about the nightjar. In the procedure, the parent washes the stone with honey beer or rice paste and water and makes this promise: "If it is true that I have touched the nightjar, then I will give you a cock and a hen if my children live." The contract is supposed to protect living children as well as those yet unborn. When the sacrificer speaks, he or she addresses the bird directly "who is always with you; wherever you go, it is over your head." The villagers do not know how the bird kills children, but they say that many mothers have lost children, made the sacrifice, and subsequently borne living progeny. At the time of the rite, when the cock and hen are killed, many people gather for dancing and a small feast in the early evening. Anyone who participates in the meal or eats from the gourd that contained the original libation is believed to become as tainted as if they had actually touched the bird. Thus, the rite serves as much to "contaminate" as it does to "cleanse," and though the bird is supposedly removed from over one head, it is given ample opportunity to find others.

An identical rite used to be performed for a married man or woman who had stepped on a certain species of black-and-red-banded caterpillar. The libation and payment were made to a stone owned by an old woman now dead; with her death the custom disappeared. The villagers still avoid this little creature, although no sacrifice has been made in its behalf by any woman of child-bearing age presently living in Tonghia. I was unable to identify this caterpillar because someone thoughtfully released the one I had collected.

Women of childbearing age do not eat eggs, pigeons, tortoises, and small red antelopes with tufted foreheads. Badyaranké women do not eat eggs because "you don't eat the child of another to nourish your own children." Also, if a woman eats the pigeon, her child may sicken and her milk dry up. This belief also works in reverse: "If you have a baby and have no milk, you remember that you have eaten a pigeon." Thus, absence of milk implies a forgotten infraction, just as infraction causes absence of milk. To cure this sickness the woman retires to the rear of the women's house where they winnow and where pigeons feed; she lies on the ground and cries like a pigeon while a man fires a rifle into the ground as if he were shooting a pigeon. A woman who has eaten the flesh of a tortoise must put a tortoise bone in the water jar from which children drink to protect them from sickness. Contamination from the little tufted red antelope is more serious, for it is thought that if a woman treads where this gentle animal has walked, or has eaten its meat, the child will become gravely ill. This sickness (*nunkorunkorun*) has symptoms which include trembling and irregular breathing, and it not infrequently terminates in death. If a woman has had contact with the animal or if her child apparently has the sickness, she goes to a hunter for treatment. At Tonghia, two men knew the treatment but did it differently; both, however, put a concoction of leaves into water, recited a verse over it, and massaged the mother or child with the solution. As additional security, the mother or the child may wear the deer's tuft because, paradoxically, this part of the animal is believed to protect against contamination. The mother may also suspend a perforated potsherd over her bed as a long-term prophylactic against the sickness. It is interesting and important that these explanations are circular: if a woman has touched the forbidden animal, her child will sicken, and if a child sickens, its mother has touched the forbidden animal.

All these avoidances apply to women in their fertile years and children who are not yet circumcised or excised are the victims of the sicknesses that are believed due to their mothers' inadvertent breaking of the taboos. Therefore, it is not surprising that young children, too, are bound by these taboos. If a young boy, for example, has eaten a pigeon, the Badyaranké believe his circumcision wound will fester and not heal because the pigeon has lodged in the penis. Conversely, if a boy develops sickness as a result of his circumcision, they know that he has eaten the pigeon, though they say that "one doesn't know if a child has eaten these until he is circumcised."

Another belief concerns vicious quarrelling which is said to create a hot and evil breeze sufficiently powerful to strike down children exposed to such an atmosphere. Although this belief does not prevent people from quarrelling, it does make quarrelling a taboo — which is often violated.

A final belief, held widely in Africa and elsewhere, concerns the postpartum sex taboo: if a husband resumes sexual intercourse with his wife within two or three years after she has had a child, her milk may be poisoned, and the child may sicken and die. This taboo was invoked during my stay in the village in two cases, although the unfortunate children had ceased drinking their mothers' milk before their illness.

In summary, there is a sizeable body of Badyaranké theory explaining infant mortality, stemming from so many causes that it would seem impossible for a woman or her child to avoid all the contaminating influences. It should also be apparent that the suffering caused by infraction of these taboos implies no mystical profiteering — no one is seen to get ahead. These taboos are more than a naive theory of disease or a philosophy of misfortune. To the Badyaranké, a personal misfortune suggests a personal cause, ordinarily in the idiom of witchcraft. These taboos provide an alternative explanation to witchcraft for an age group where sickness is common and death too familiar.

LIFE AFTER DEATH

The Badyaranké are not preoccupied with thinking about life after death, and their beliefs relating to ghosts and ancestors are uncomplicated. They speak of another world (*lakire*) which contrasts with this world (*dunya*). Kodan controls both of these and resides in paradise (*ardiana*) where he is served by angels (*malaika*). Hell (*dyname*) is said to be inhabited by the devil (*ibulisse*) who is served by lesser devils (*satani*) who receive the damned (*kafri*). Most of these terms are traceable to Arabic, except the term for God itself, which is distinctly Badyaranké.

An individual, say the Badyaranké, goes to heaven or hell depending on his behavior in this life. Man possesses a personality (*dyiko*) which appears after birth, ends at death, and may change during his lifetime. The soul (*watyi*) comes from Kodan and is eventually collected by him; and all death, regardless of intermediate causes, is initiated by him. This high deity is otherwise removed from human affairs. Ancestors are known as the grandparents (*bemame*). Ghosts (*ubudisé*) are thought to exist but to be timid and rare, and to have no relations with living people. The word for ghost is comparable to the English *spook*: it can refer to anything frightening or eerie. The word for religion (*dina*) refers specifically to Islam. No word in Badyaranké corresponds to *supernatural*. An informant whom I questioned about these matters said, "This isn't important — we work and we eat."

THE GREAT SERPENT

Another supernatural creature should be mentioned: the fabulous giant serpent (*ninkinanka*), which was first described by Beatrice Appia in 1944 and later by Monique de Lestrange in 1950. The giant serpent is believed to live in great rivers and to leave its watery abode on Fridays, especially during the wet months; when it travels on land, the rains fall, lights glitter from its head, and all the drums, bells, and radios of the village give out music. Badyaranké say it resembles a python and if, by accident, it is seen by someone, that person dies. This serpent retired into the rivers at an unknown time in the past because it feared men would kill it. Two men are supposed to have seen it: one watched for an entire morning as half of the serpent passed by, and the other watched during the afternoon as the posterior half passed by. Both men are said to have died within two days of this event.

A second, less fabulous serpent (*tyasumpé*) is said to be an intermediate being between the giant serpent and the python. In this hierarchy, an old python may become a tyasumpé, and an old tyasumpé may become a giant serpent. This lesser creature is believed to live in smaller streams and springs. On one occasion, a hunter from Tonghia claimed he killed a tyasumpé and that it required eleven men to carry part of it back to the village. (This same hunter, who is a seer, told me matter-of-factly

71

that his father lived more than a thousand years.) It is said in the village that a little boy fell out of a mango tree and broke his arm because of this killing.

SUMMARY

The Badyaranké believe that Kodan and the village genies communicate with the villagers through a time-honored system of regular, reciprocal exchanges, and do not engage in short-term contractual arrangements. Men never expect to reverse their inferior status vis-à-vis these powers, but through periodic sacrifices and occasional emergency offerings they maintain good rapport with them.

The powers available for individual manipulation — shrines, matrisib ancestors, Islamic and pagan magic — do not favor matrisib elders (sib seniority, available only to women, is determined by age and is not of political importance), nor do they favor the village chief or compound headman (neither status confers great authority, and both may be aspired to by any male, except in the case of blacksmiths who are sometimes excluded from chieftainship). Equality of access to these statuses in Badyaranké society is paralleled by equality of access to the publicly manipulatable supernatural powers. In accordance with the minor advantages which these statuses confer, the advantages gained through the use of these powers are no greater for a chief than for a commoner. In both cases, individuals are free to make the effort necessary to assure continued good fortune, to improve their fortune, and to obtain fleeting and minor advantages over other people. The Badyaranké do not contradict Mary Douglas's suggestion that "there may be a correlation between explicit authority and controlled spiritual power." [4]

Although a marabout's knowledge and a shrine may be engaged by a person to cause another harm, the Badyaranké do not think that such use is absolutely wrong, but that the rightness or wrongness depends upon the individual's judgment concern-

[4] 1966:101.

ing the merit of what these powers are used for. This use generally involves the righting of a real or imagined injustice.

On the other hand, it is believed that powers associated with the numerous taboos may not be coerced into responding to the demands of individuals or groups, and thus rites or spells to influence them cannot be learned. No one and nothing is seen to profit either materially or mystically from their influence, and no one is punished for the suffering caused by the infraction of taboos. They simply intrude into people's destinies.

## CHAPTER FOUR

*Internal Powers:*
*The Seer*

## THE SOUL

The Badyaranké believe that the soul was given by God in heaven, through both the mother and the father, and at death the soul returns to the sky (God and the sky are synonymous in Badyaranké). People are said to differ, however, in the properties of their souls. Some souls are considered to be heavy, spherical, and slippery; they cannot be separated from the body except briefly, and then at the risk of death. People with such souls are referred to in Badyaranké as *umadure* (non-seer). Other souls are said to be lighter, more agile, and easier to grasp; these may depart from the body at will for long periods of time. People with these souls are called umadisé (seer). The Badyaranké concept of umadisé [1] has no parallel in English, and the discovery of its

---

[1] Similar concepts exist among the Wolof, Manding, Fula Kunda, and Peul Fouta — also perhaps among the Coniagui and Bassari.

meaning and usages became the most absorbing focus of my inquiries during the latter months of fieldwork.

The power of the seer is said to be inherent, and is inherited from either or both parents. If only one parent has the power, the child may be born a non-seer; it cannot possess the power if neither of its parents are seers; the child exercises no choice over which of the two kinds of souls it will receive. Umadisé is an involuntary state that can neither be learned nor unlearned, and may be possessed by both men and women.

How do the Badyaranké distinguish a seer? A person might suspect another of being a seer if his head is "pointed" or big, if he has a restless and nervous disposition, or if, as a child, he walked by the village elders without showing awkwardness or fear. It is said that the bark of a certain tree (known in Badyaranké as *matyaké*) when powdered and mixed with water causes the seer who drinks it to vomit. These are but tenuous ways of recognizing seers, available to non-seers.

All seers possess what Badyaranké describe as the "eyes of the night" (*masse padiena*) by which one seer recognizes another. The eyes of the night are said to lie below, and lateral to, the ordinary eyes and are invisible to non-seers. With these eyes, the seer witnesses a dimension inhabited by genies (dyinné), sprites (ufann and *foncoté*), and various secret objects and animals which the non-seer believes to exist but cannot observe himself.

Badyaranké believe that a seer may intentionally disassociate his soul from his body and transform it into anything in nature. Thus, he may be in two places at once; his body may be seen by ordinary people while his soul wanders; and the transformed soul, too, may be seen by non-seers. Since a seer may change himself into anything, a Badyaranké is never sure whether a whirlwind, animal, insect, or tree might be someone. A risk which a seer runs when he changes into an animal is that he will die at once if the animal is slain, or shortly thereafter. A seer is said to have the capability to withstand pain because, when threatened, he may invest his soul in another person (possibly the one who beats him), so that individual feels the blows. Another indication

75

is that a young boy who is a seer can, by willing it, prevent a blacksmith's knife from penetrating his foreskin at circumcision.

An additional attribute said to be possessed by the seer is his ability to transcend conventional limitations of time and space by travelling enormous distances in an instant. He may observe events as they happen far away, and his dreams are believed to be a more reliable preview of the future than are the dreams of non-seers. He cannot, according to my information, enter the past or the future.

Another ability of seers is shown in this example: if two young men agree to cultivate a peanut field together and one of them is a seer, he may rise early in the morning and turn the tree stumps into workers, so that when his colleague arrives, he will be astonished by the amount of work that his partner has accomplished in so little time. The Badyaranké are sensitive about each doing his share in cooperative endeavors; from this illustration, the suspicion arises that a person who does more than his share might be considered to be a seer by his neighbors.

Some seers are said to be more powerful than others; the most powerful of all are capable of seeing the most senior of the genies without fear. These upper limits of power are considered extremely dangerous and potentially self-destructive, and may cause insanity. A powerful seer is thought to have seen too much to retain control of his perceptions — he no longer follows the call of human society because he hears another measure, perhaps that of the genies, far away.

In addition to some humans, the seer category includes genies, sprites, and a number of animals. One informant asserted that all animals are seers, but then denied that fish or lizards could have this power. The little tufted antelope (considered so dangerous to women and children) is said to be a seer, and the two black glandular discolorations on his snout to be his eyes of the night. This same designation is made for the two spongy red lobes inside the skull of the catfish, although several informants denied that such creatures could be seers.

Badyaranké thought on the psychic attributes of animals is unsystematic and does not reveal much deliberate concern. The transformation of animals into human or other forms, although believed possible, is seldom if ever thought to occur.

The senior blacksmith of Tonghia, one of my closest friends and principal sources of information, told two tales about animals and an anvil which were seers:

On the route to Patin Kouta there was a white crocodile who lived in a hole. It was said that this crocodile was a blacksmith and that the hole belonged to porcupines. When a hunter went to the hole at night to await the porcupine, he would dream that a white crocodile came out of the hole. One runs from this crocodile, although it is said no longer to be there, and can only be seen in a dream. Those who have seen it have said that the crocodile was a blacksmith. One does not want to admit that he has actually seen it; one says that he dreamed to conceal the fact that he is a seer since the crocodile can only be seen by a seer. He protects the porcupines. A now dead blacksmith from the compound of Cayimo saw the white crocodile.

To the south of the village of Tonghia in an abandoned field is an anvil that no one can take. It is older than the village. One does not know what lives there, but there is something. It is made of iron but not everyone can see it. He who last saw it is now dead. He was a blacksmith and he was a seer. No one has ever been heard working on the anvil.

The response to the question of whether the seer category included Kodan was, "No one knows if God is a seer or not." The question was thought to be irrelevant.

LIMINAL RITES: CIRCUMCISION AND DEATH

Despite Badyaranké theory that the seer's power is permanent and hereditary, there are revealing contradictions to this in practice. Young boys are frequently thought to be seers during the one or two months following their circumcision, and for this reason certain features of the rite are described below.

The date for circumcision is determined by the elders, generally early in the dry season (January or February), every two or three years, or whenever there are three or more boys between the ages of about seven to ten whom their fathers consider ready. On the morning of the chosen day the young candidates are led by a procession of male elders to a clearing south of the village. There they are lined up, undressed, and circumcised by blacksmiths, with a frenzied background of musket fire and bull-roarers. The boys are subsequently divided into two groups, according to the side of the village to which they belong, and are led off to two secret camps in the bush, that for Satian to the east of the village and that for Bantasu to the west. Each camp is guarded by a seer who remains with the boys throughout the duration of their isolation, which generally lasts from five to six weeks. During this period the boys are taught obedience to elders, secret knowledge, and rules of behavior toward women, who are forbidden to visit or even look at them.

On several occasions while the newly circumcised boys are confined to their bush camps, two masked dancers (*concurra*), one from each camp, enter the village. Boys and young men who have already been circumcised shred a certain red bark with which they cover the entire body of one among them. The bark-covered dancer then leads a troop of boys (except those just circumcised) into the village to assault female property and to beat the women's houses with axes, sabres, and clubs. The women barricade themselves within their houses and are forbidden to lay eyes upon the concurra.

The masked dancer is said not to be a person, but rather to be "something of the bush," and this "something" is a seer (umadisé). He frightens and punishes the women for any filth there may be in the village, and before the dancer arrives, the women very industriously sweep everything. He also has the right to insult or even beat anyone, male or female, thought to be engaged in witchcraft. Any young man who wishes to do so may wear the mask in the assault, and the mask once discarded has no power. But the being created when the mask is worn has the ability to shriek in an undecipherable language and the power to see the world of the night.

It is thought that witches [2] are especially avid for the soul of a

---

[2] A witch is a seer who uses his powers for evil purposes. Witches are thought to cause death by invisible psychic means and to eat the victim's soul. See page 96.

newly circumcised boy, and for that reason the boys are under the tutelage of seers. Witches desire the newly circumcised boys' souls because their guardians present a challenge to the powers of witchery, and they would like to overcome the seer in whose mystical powers the village has entrusted its next generation of young men. Thus, again a circular reasoning is apparent: witches desire the souls of the newly circumcised because they are guarded; and the boys are guarded because the witches want their souls. Various amulets are made by the blacksmiths and by fathers of the boys to protect their bodies from witches. Outside the camp limits, protection for the boys while they gather firewood is provided by bull-roarers which are believed capable of clearing witches (as well as women) from the forest paths as the boys file along, clad in blue cotton robes, with firewood on their heads.

When their wounds are considered healed, they are led to the village center from the two camps, dressed in elaborate regalia that includes women's handkerchiefs and jewelry; then for several nights they dance in the midst of much festivity. Each boy is allowed to sleep with any mature unmarried girl who desires him, for two or three nights; congress is said not to occur. Thus the boys have made the transition from *posé*, which resembles the word *child* or *kid*, to *wambani*, which means *boy*. Circumcision is a rite of passage that confers sexuality on sexually undifferentiated children. When their female trappings which they have worn since their return from camp finally wear out, they are considered fully male.

Like newly circumcised boys becoming seers for a short time, corpses during the period before burial, too, were believed to be umadisé. Until about twenty years ago, a relative of the deceased could request that the corpse be given an opportunity to indicate its killer if witchcraft was thought to be involved in the death. In such a case, all the men of the village went to a clearing where a path divided, and sat in a circle on the ground. An elder interrogated the corpse, which was wrapped in a hammock and suspended between two men; he asked the corpse if anyone present was responsible for the death, and if so, to point out the witch by swinging its head toward him. The Badyaranké say that if the elder himself had "eaten the soul," the corpse would have indicated this before his question was finished; if one of the bearers had been responsible, both bearers would have been unable to budge in any direction, for their movements were controlled by the power within the corpse; and if the corpse had paused in front of a women's house, those within would have been required to present themselves for its scrutiny.

In contrast to a non-seer becoming a seer for the brief period after death, a seer apparently loses his power during this time. If, for example, a hunter killed an animal that had behaved peculiarly or perhaps died too easily, he might suspect it was a transformed seer. The Badyaranké of Tonghia tell of a hunter in Guinea who had strangled a panther to death, a nearly impossible task. The panther was then wrapped in a hammock and told, "If you are a real panther, show us the man who killed you." The bearers walked to where the hunter was hiding and singled him out. Had the panther been a transformed seer, it would not have been able to identify its killer.

THE STRANGERS WITHIN: THE BLACKSMITHS

All blacksmiths are thought to be seers, and by virtue of this power, they work fearlessly with fire and have the task of circumcising the young boys. Ideally, blacksmithing techniques and tools are passed from father to son. If a father dies before he can teach his son the trade, the lad learns it through an older brother, or even a distantly related smith, with whom he lives and works.

All smiths, with some rare exceptions, bear the patronymic Kamara, and it is said that formerly all Kamaras were smiths, had non-Badyaranké origins, and were required to marry among themselves. For an unknown period of time, the smiths have failed to observe endogamy, but it is considered a duty for a master smith to give his daughter in marriage to an apprentice and if he has no daughter, to give him an anvil. Of twenty-four consummated or prospective marriages of blacksmiths at Tonghia, six unions were between apprentices and their master's daughters; thus, to a limited extent, smiths may be regarded as an endogamous occupational descent group. Blacksmiths tend to live to gether in the same compounds, each with its workshed at the village center; at Tonghia, twelve smiths lived in three compounds, each having a shed.

The smiths claim that everyone is their joking partner. If they install a new anvil or repair their sheds, they have the right to appropriate palm wine, honey beer, and building materials from anyone in the village. They also say they have the right to insult anyone, including the village chief. The smiths' privileged status in this respect differs from the previously described joking relationship in that it is nonreciprocal. In actual practice, however, the smiths no longer appropriate property at will and are much less privileged than these dated norms suggest.

If someone has cheated, insulted, or denied food and drink to a smith, he may be refused service by all the smiths of the village until he has apologized. On two occasions remembered at Tonghia, the smiths quarrelled with the chief, and the entire village was denied access to the forge until the appropriate amends were made.

The most potent sanction available to the Badyaranké in their interminable disputes with the nomads is to forbid them access to the smith's services, thus obliging the nomads to travel great distances in order to purchase needed tools. This sanction was exercised twice during my visit. On one occasion, the Fula Kunda village of Akan made an independent arrangement with a truck owner to transport its peanut crop to a town where it could be sold for a higher price than in the bush. This broke an agreement the Akan villagers had with the Tonghia people to market their peanuts together, and the Akan people were forbidden to visit any of the three forges in Tonghia. Whether or not the Badyaranké of Tonghia are justified in terms of Senegalese law, they are usually able to have the last word in these intervillage disputes because of the great inconvenience they can create by refusing to provide iron tools.

Whenever a distribution of items is to be made, the smiths are called upon to allocate portions to each individual. When the chief receives his stipend from the Government, the smiths divide it between the compounds of the village according to their relative sizes. If the Fula Kunda bring a gift of palm wine or meat to the village, the smiths normally determine its partition. This function of the smiths is most important in rituals: the redistribution of kola nuts after the circumcision or funeral ceremonies, or in any gatherings where quantities of kola nuts and rice paste are reallocated. It is also said that smiths may be called upon to divide the items in a case of disputed inheritance.

The Badyaranké think that the two roles of chief and smith should not be invested in a single individual if this can be avoided; thus, blacksmiths are, as a rule, excluded from the chieftainship. In some small villages of only one or two compounds where most of the inhabitants are blacksmiths, there are exceptions. But, in general, the role of chief as collector and that of the blacksmith as distributor are kept apart. (If the Fula Kunda were to give the village chief some game, they would give him the shoulders because, like the chief, "they come first"; if meat were given a blacksmith, however, the portion would be the rump "because he works on his rump." The smiths are said to know the needs of each compound and individual, and their judgment is believed to be objective and final. The chief conceivably is vulnerable to criticism for any inequalities of distribution, but the smiths are immune, and thereby relieve the chief of a potentially controversial task.

Blacksmiths, their wives, and children have a special avoidance relationship with the python. To touch this serpent, or even to tread where it has passed, is supposed to invite sickness, running sores, and miscellaneous bad luck, which can be cured only by a sacrifice to the anvil. On one occasion that I know of at Tonghia, a man who had been a smith, but had abandoned the trade, shot and killed a python that threatened his chickens. Within the year, his compound burned completely and he had open sores on his shins. To him there was no question but that his misfortunes originated from the python.

In summary, the blacksmiths are thought to be of non-Badyaranké origin in very ancient times, are somewhat endogamous today, were more so in the past, and are normally excluded from

Top, *a hunter in traditional Badyaranké dress; bottom, a close-up of a blacksmith at work, with his anvil lying left of center, in front of his right foot.*

chieftainship. They enjoy a certain amount of license, and exercise less fallible judgment than most in distributions of property and the disputes originating therefrom. Finally, they are believed to be in more or less constant touch with the world of the night.

## GENIES AND SPRITES

The seer is believed to be able to engage in a number of patterned interactions with the genies and sprites. He may — secretly, alone, and at night — approach the genies to ask for wealth or good fortune. The following two accounts illustrate the hazards encountered in using this avenue.

For him who wants to be important, there is a place at Combo, a village of Combonké in Gambia. It is difficult because you kill a cow there alone and wait until night when the genies come. At nightfall the smallest genie comes first. You aren't frightened of these, so next come the young men, and so on, until the oldest genies come with their spears. They stick you with these to make you afraid. They ask you what you want. Some people run away, others go crazy, others can't talk. If you can talk, you say, "I want to be a chief," or "I want money." If you continue to talk straight, you get what you want. If you start rambling, it's all finished. There are some who lose control of what they say, and ask for weeds and bushes, and these grow everywhere, even in their houses.

On the mountain of Badyar, in Guinea, you go at night for magic. You take off all your clothes until you are naked. Then the chief of the genies sends the python and all the most dangerous serpents. You undress at a certain place and the serpent comes and rolls around you. He walks all over you. If you have no fear he descends and goes. The chief himself comes. He spits fire. He asks you what you want. You say, "Money," "Intelligence," whatever, and he gives that, and you go back home. If you are a child when you see the chief of the genies, you go mad. It is necessary to be older. This is only for men. The genies are still there, but men now don't dare go to see them.

The Badyaranké believe it is not always necessary to confront a genie in his lair to obtain his treasure, for individuals may steal belongings of the genies as a means to improve well-being. One of three consequences is said to follow if a person has stolen from a genie: he will succeed; he will be caught by the genie and sicken; or he will be caught by the genie and die. The following stories from my fieldnotes show these consequences.

If one goes to a compound of genies and one is a seer, he sees that they have beads, drumsticks, hats, etc. He who wants to be a good drummer can take the sticks and he will be a champion. The genies leave a little genie to guard these things. If someone has stolen from them, they ask the little genie who it was, and then they follow him. If they find the culprit, they knock him down and he trembles and cries. They try to open his fist to retrieve what he stole. If it is in the hand, they take it back and that's all. If he swallowed it, however, they enter inside him and this causes death. If one isn't a seer, one can't see the property of the genies.

Several years ago, a stranger came to Tonghia who had stolen something from a genie. He came to the village and the people shaved his head so that the genies couldn't recognize him. The next morning he was well. But the genies came that next evening while he slept. They opened and closed the door several times and then threw a stone against the man's leg and broke it. But the man was unaware of this until the next morning, when he couldn't stand up. Two days later he died. He had swallowed what he had taken. This was the second time he stole from the genies. The first time, his Koranic teacher returned the article for him.

One man who wanted to be important took the hat of a genie and changed himself into a baby. He buried the hat in the sand and sat on it. The genie came and said, "Has someone passed by?" and the baby nodded yes. The genie asked the contrary and again the baby nodded yes. The genie finally said, "This is only a child who doesn't know anything." When the genie departed, the man went to another country and became a chief there.

Nokoli, the senior hunter of the village of Tonghia, was stricken with a trembling sickness in 1964. It was said that he had stolen the musket balls of a genie, and that was why he was sick.

In this interaction, a seer steals something from the genie and, depending on what he has stolen, will obtain great proficiency or wealth, providing he avoids discovery. The stolen object can be returned by a marabout who knows how to deal with genies through the *savoir* (knowledge) of his Koran, or it can be returned by a blacksmith who is in rapport with the genies. In the last story above, sickness provided the rationale for Nokoli's being a good hunter: he was being punished by the genies whose bullets had temporarily profited him. Talent in any particular activity, if gained through the genie's consent or through sleight of hand at the genie's expense, is a precarious gift that invites sickness and death. Annihilation can be part and parcel of success.

This logic may also work in reverse. A woman of Tonghia who is now mad, is rumored to have been very wealthy before her madness. Being unable to learn of any tangible elements of her wealth, I attribute the rumor to an attitude that since she is now mad, she once must have been wealthy.

There also exists a variety of standardized interactions with genies that do not require the person to be a seer. The Badyaranké believe that genies may clandestinely impregnate women, who subsequently give birth to children who are not human, "but something of the bush." One informant was unsure whether such impregnation was caused by genies or by sprites. A woman is said to risk impregnation by genies if she copulates in the bush rather than in the village, or if she undresses by a stream to wash at midday or at dusk, the hours when women should be working in the village, and when the streams and rice fields are vacant. If a woman has intercourse with a man in the bush, a genie may profit from her exposure and seize the man from within, obliging him to request the services of a marabout to separate them. Genies may even try to profit if a woman copulates during the day in the village. In all cases, the genitals are exposed at odd times or places. The Badyaranké say a genie enters the woman as an invisible serpent or as a toothed insect, and if he discovers a child already in the woman's womb, he kills it and takes its place.

The bizarre children which are the supposed results of such unions are considered to be seers and to be dangerous. The child of a genie father and human mother is usually born with obvious visible characteristics like a lopsided head, or absence of ears, nose, or genitals. Such children born with teeth are said to be particularly dangerous. Unlike other seers, their "eyes of the night" are supposedly not inherited from their mothers, but from genies. Although such children are often called small sprites (foncoté), not all small sprites are said to be conceived in this way. When a sprite child is born, it is killed, ideally by a black-smith and his assistant, with a musket and a hammer in the bush. These accounts of sprite-children were collected at Tonghia.

In Guinea, a woman gave birth to a monster. A man named Moussa was given the responsibility for killing it. Tonto, the son of Moussa, said, "I want to come." The father said, "You can't come; this is serious." The child secretly followed his father. The father took the monster and hit it with a hammer in the bush. The monster elongated and took Moussa by the head. The son of Moussa came out of hiding, elongated even more than the monster, and beat it on the head; the monster died. The son said to his father, "Now you know why I wanted to come."

The wife of a man of Tonghia gave birth to a monster child. If she carried the child on her back, it elongated. Its head was twisted, and it flicked its tongue like a serpent. They told the mother to bring the baby to a path in the bush and leave it there. Then a young blacksmith and a man from the woman's compound killed and buried it.

At Paonka, the wife of a hunter gave birth to a monster. The hunter put the child in a honey-collecting basket, sealed it, and brought it to the bush where he burned it. This hunter was a seer.

Another type of relation people have with genies is outright possession by them. A man — or a woman — is thought to be possessed by genies if he has incurable wounds, or especially if he displays nervous trembling, fits, or madness. Of numerous cases of people in Tonghia believed to be under the control of genies, these next examples show the range of this phenomenon. One adult woman has been delirious for several years and has a running sore that no medicine has healed; several marabouts have divined that this woman "has a genie." A healthy young woman, now living in her mother's brother's compound, had two husbands who died; a third man who inherited her abandoned her for fear that he too would die; she learned from a marabout that she has something, probably a genie, in her head. A middle-aged married woman had a history of hysterical seizures when she gave birth, which were thought to be caused by a genie who also took the children's lives; he was driven away by some injections she received at a hospital in Guinea. An aged woman has suffered from a festering foot for several years because, it is thought, a genie in the form of a snake has entered the wound.

A so-called false genie (*cougnadia*) may come to startle a sleeper, though not to take possession.

He can come in, even if the door is closed, to seize you. You wake up but you can't move. He beats you and you cry, but no one can hear you. You think you can be heard but you can't. As long as you can't move, he stays. As soon as you can move a finger, he goes. If you are sleeping with someone and that someone touches you, he goes also. After the false genie tires you, you must change your sleeping position or he will come back. If you place a knife or a fire by your head, he can't come. He just comes to annoy.

The genies are believed to play a variety of other tricks on unsuspecting humans. Both genies and small sprites supposedly can exchange anatomical parts with a person — preferably a child. For example, a genie with knock-knees may give these to a child in return for the child's straight legs, and the child thereafter bears the stigma of walking on genie's legs. People of Tonghia tell of an ill-tempered genie who lived in a tree and who gave goitre to several people in a compound near his house. Some of them cured their goitre by conventional magic, and one young man who was a seer said he passed his on to a dog. In another instance, a genie may wish to participate in a particular celebration, and does so, typically, in the form of a beautiful girl who is never seen again.

In relations between seers and genies, a seer always initiates the interaction. The seer either gains or loses, or sometimes both; but the genie gains little or nothing. Relations between non-seers and genies differ in that they are always genie-initiated. In this role, the genie acts as a trickster. A person may be feared or disliked because he "has a genie," but the genie is apparently indifferent in his choice of host. Thus, genies provide the Badyaranké with explanations for certain kinds of nervous and mental illnesses, some incurable wounds, some deaths, and much of what an American might call luck.

88

Before concluding the discussion of genies, their role as owners of the soil should be mentioned. To make a new Badyaranké village or compound, the persons involved must first make peace with the genies, and renew this peace thereafter with sacrifices. To clear a new field from the bush, a man might, for example, bury a certain type of bean in the earth, and if on the next day the beans were disinterred, it would mean the genie-owner had refused permission. If the man does not seek the genie's consent or proceeds to clear the field despite his refusal, that man will have poor health, a bad field, and probably a short life.

Genies supposedly live very much like people and require permission before their resources can be exploited. If a person defecates in a clearing in the bush, and returns the next day to find the feces gone, this disappearance may indicate the location of a family of genies; if he defecates again in the same spot, the genies may drive him away. Even such a minor occurrence as a loss of balance while walking along a forest path may, to a villager, be an instance of genie-at-work — perhaps genies had spread their grain out to dry in the sun, and did not want the passerby to step on their food.

A person may protect himself against genie-initiated bad luck by using marabout prescriptions, Koranic waters, and written amulets. The traditional prophylactics include beads made from the root of a certain bush, the large red beans from a wild vine, and the leaves of a small parasitic plant that grows at the base of the millet stalk.

The long-legged sprite (ufann) is considered to be less awesome, fearful, and powerful than the genies. He lives in the forest, the streams, or the fields, and comes to the village on invitation only. Ufann is said to resemble a man nine or ten meters tall, with long legs, a tiny head, and huge ears, and to speak a peculiar language that can sometimes be heard trumpeting from damp recesses in the forest where he hides. Widely known as a petty thief who steals honey, ufann is said to walk behind the collector and drink the sweet from the gourd carried on his head. The Badyaranké say that if palm wine is foamy and dirty, the big sprite may have washed his hands in it. Ufann acts as guardian of edible and portable resources, both in the bush and in the village. In this role he can be approached by seers, or he can approach them, to agree to a contract whereby the seer will kill much game, trap many fish, grow much grain, or earn much money. In most circumstances, one must be a seer to see and communicate with ufann. In two cases, the long-legged sprite was seen by groups of people: a party of men fishing, and several men walking along a path.

Contracts are made with ufann by men, not women, because they are more concerned with the resources he controls. Generally, this sprite demands a human life to guarantee his part of the contract. A man making the agreement confers a human life to the sprite simply by giving him permission to take a particular individual. The following passages from informants illustrate how ufann is said to enter into relations with seers.

There are people who capture the big sprite [ufann] and put him in their granary. If you keep him in the granary, the millet is never exhausted, but every three years it is necessary to give him a human life. The hunter also befriends the sprite and thereafter the animals die easily for him. But each time the hunter has a child, he must give it to the sprite. The big sprite eats the people given him. The big sprite knows if someone desires his services. He comes to the man and says, "Are you looking for me?" and the man says, "Yes." The sprite says, "Each year you give me a person." The man says, "That is too much, but each year I can give you a dog." The sprite then refuses, and the man says that the sprite demands too much. Then they bargain some more, and they decide that every three years the man will give him a person. Thereafter, all that the man searches for in the village he will find. The sprite takes from other people's granaries to give to the man.

One of the founders of Tonghia kept a big sprite in his granary. He found the sprite during a battle with the Fula Kunda. Because of the shooting, the sprite ran out of the bushes. He captured the sprite, brought it back to his compound, and put it in his granary. Each year he gave it a sheep. This is not good because the sprite steals from the granaries of others to keep that of his host full. When the elder died, his son inherited the sprite. The son gave both of his wives to the sprite. The sprite once attacked another woman of the compound in the form of a cat. After the son died, the sprite ran back into the bush.

The big sprite surveys his resources. If one gives him nothing, he interferes. One can't make a fish trap in the river that passes through the rice field of Tonghia, because the sprite there says he can't give lots of rice and lots of fish, too.

Every several years, someone at Tonghia takes the initiative to ask the villagers to help him construct a fish weir in a nearby river. The owner of the fish weir then passes a great deal of time by himself in the forest catching fish. The villagers automatically assume that if the fisherman's catches are bountiful, he has made a contract with the sprite, and if the catches are poor, he has refused to do so. In 1965, a young man who had built a weir caught few fish, and one night the weir collapsed. In Badyaranké eyes, he had clearly refused to meet the sprite's terms, and the sprite had destroyed his fishing apparatus. Several years earlier, a visitor made a weir, caught many fish, left the village on a trip, and died soon afterwards. Again, it was clear to the villagers that he had made a contract with the sprite and ran away before he paid his part of the bargain; the sprite in return took the fisherman's life.

Although there are numerous tales concerning persons who keep sprites, only one resident of Tonghia (to my knowledge) was reported to have recently possessed ufann. Wopar has been the best cultivator, the richest cash-cropper, and generally the most acquisitive and affluent member of the village, as is testified by his peanut sales receipts, his large well-kept compound, and his four wives. Throughout his life he has frequently been criticized by others in his compound for alleged neglect of collective labor. When one of the men with whom Wopar quarrelled became ill, the man's son declared that his father was being preyed upon by a sprite who was collecting payments for making an unspecified someone wealthy. Now that Wopar is in his sixties, and his health and physical vigor — and thus his fortune — are declining, it is rumored that the sprite has left. Before having heard of his suspected flirtation with the world of the night, I once asked Wopar what he knew about ufann — to which he replied, "What! Me! How do I know about that? I don't know anything about such things. Ha!"

In summary, the evidence of prosperity contains within it the possibility that it was achieved through the expenditure of other people's lives. Ufann would probably applaud George Foster's "image of limited good" which describes a world where " 'the pie is constant in size' . . . if someone is seen to get ahead, logically it can only be at the expense of others in the village" [3] as an accurate appraisal of those aspects of the economy which he controls. The sprite does not create resources, but keeps his host provided for by stealing from others. It is said that the contractor generally pays with the lives of those who eat the grain, fish, or meat acquired thereby. Although the contract with the sprite is considered bad, a person is not punished for it, as he would be for witchcraft. Beliefs about sprites would not prevent a Badyaranké from accumulating wealth, but they do give those who do not a source of gossip and, perhaps more important, a sense of righteousness in being ordinary.

Two other men in the village, although nearly as wealthy as Wopar, never seemed to be suspected of harboring sprites. These two men live in atypical, small compounds with their own spouses and dependents — not in large, extended family compounds. Perhaps an individual is more likely to be suspected of keeping a sprite if he lives and works with a large number of people, in a situation where the difference between private and collective interests is more important. To speculate, then, freedom from the interdependency of large compounds is associated with freedom from suspicion that the individual's success is gained at the expense of others, which may in a real, if not mystical sense, be true.

Some villagers affirm while others deny that the small sprite (foncoté) engages in contracts. He is said to be weaker and more timid than ufann, and therefore a less coveted provider. He had been described as small and hairy, with a large, cloven head that he acquired when he once barred the route between two villages. The foncoté supposedly challenged passersby to fight, and he always won until one day a blacksmith appeared who asked the sprite to hit him. The sprite replied, "No, you hit me first," so the blacksmith knocked him over the head with a heavy iron

[3] Foster 1960:177.

bar which he had concealed up his sleeve. Since that time, the small sprite has been timid and satisfies himself by making noises at night, frightening people in the forest, and scurrying aimlessly. Some children at Tonghia reported that foncoté was fond of throwing pebbles on the corrugated iron roof of the schoolhouse which they attend in a nearby village.

## ACCUSED AND ADMITTED SEERS

Elsewhere in Africa, as well as in some other parts of the world, men who succeed too well risk being identified with potentially dangerous mystical powers.[4] Among the Tiv of Nigeria, described by Laura and Paul Bohannan, men of influence and probity are generally men with *tsav*, or witchcraft substance. The Nyakyusa, who live across the continent in Tanzania, perform a ritual to assure that village headmen will possess a mystical "python power" with which they protect their subjects from harm.[5]

Successful individuals among the Badyaranké, however, deny that they are seers, and derive no advantage from being suspected as having a seer's capabilities. Furthermore, I never learned of any attempts by living villagers to enter into commerce with genies or sprites. Although *accused* is too strong a word, it will serve to distinguish between seers who are created by opinion (which responds to their behavior) and other seers, described below, who tacitly or frankly admit that they have the power. At Tonghia there are four admitted seers, in addition to blacksmiths, about whom the following biographical details were gathered.

Mamadou is one of the most intelligent men in the village, but extremely homely, dirty, and apparently impotent. He once married a half-crazy, illegitimate daughter of a Badyaranké and a Fula Kunda, but even she left him after a few months. Mamadou has been unable to secure a second wife, although he has persistently sought one. He is liked in the village, but his opinion counts for nothing at the meeting of the elders. Although he is a Moslem, he is well versed in arcane knowledge of Badyaranké culture.

[4] Bailey 1964:115; Basso 1969:54; Colson 1966:224; Foster 1965:293–315.
[5] Wilson 1951:91–135.

With Paiti (another seer, described below), he prepares the meal held after a village sacrifice because, as he says, no one is ahead of him in the village and they can count on him. For the same reasons, he generally guards the circumcision camp of the eastern half of the village. He would not have accepted this task if he did not believe he was a seer.

Chief Waliba says that Mamadou is a transient and that he is chosen to guard the circumcision camp because he would not be missed in the village: "Most often the people who guard the circumcision camp are people who are nothing, negative elements in the village, who have no other use than to guard the camp. Village affairs can go on in their absence." Waliba affirmed in the same breath that such guardians must be seers.

Mamadou told me that he has seen the large and small sprites on several occasions and described their behavior. Because he admits this and because he is trustworthy (and perhaps because he has gained nothing through these contacts), he is not suspected of ever having made agreements with them.

Moussa, a young man, did not grow as rapidly as his age-mates did, and is identified with men and boys much younger than himself, whom he resembles because of his youthful appearance and stunted size. Moussa admits that he is in rapport with the genies, although he has never sought favors from them.

Kuku lives with his wife, mother-in-law, and two small children in a small, poor, dilapidated compound. He is liked by the other villagers but is considered to be a dreamer, a poor cultivator, and a bad financial risk. For example, he owes a wealthy relative a sizeable amount of money that no one expects him to return. He often disappears into the forest at night to hunt, and has told of many unusual things he has seen. Once, he says, he managed to escape from an attack by a panther through his ability to fly. Clearly Kuku has never used his powers to improve himself at anyone's expense.

Paiti is one of the poorest cultivators in the village, generally lacks the money to buy kola nuts or tobacco, and is often drunk. Waliba said that Paiti is one of the least important elders and that meetings can easily go on without him. As in the case of Mamadou, he helps prepare the sacrificial meals and generally guards the circumcision camp for the western half of the village.

Paiti has supposedly proven his powers on a number of occasions. Once, after he had "stolen" a wife from a distant village, he was attacked by a big black bird that tried to kill him; he beat the bird which he believed was her aggrieved husband and allowed it to flee. When Woko searched for a young man's soul in a mango tree (see Case 18, page 136), Paiti helped discover where the soul was hidden. Paiti also said he recognized that an iron kettle was a young man and exposed the fact that he had come in that form to kill his younger brother at the circumcision camp. An informant said, "Paiti is known to be a seer because of talk among others in the village who have the eyes and know." IIis father, a famous hunter, was also a seer.

In several respects, the four admitted seers are diminished or incomplete people. Although wealthy men deny association with affairs of the night, these diminished men apparently desire it, and may acquire a certain importance, especially in ritual or crisis situations. They are elevated by the stigma that frequently attaches to success.

What then do blacksmiths, who are believed to be seers and who publicly perform tasks that only seers can perform, have in common with the four seers just described? In light of the beliefs that smiths derive from an alien people, were once a separate caste, and preferably should not serve as village chiefs, they may be considered diminished with respect to their participation in Badyaranké society. Unlike other admitted seers, however, their mystical attributes are inherited occupational characteristics and not a consequence of events in their individual careers. Badyaranké theory does assume that the power of all seers is hereditary, which seems inconsistent. If some individual through being rich or through admitting having powers is believed to be a seer, it is for reasons that can best be understood in terms of his own personality and behavior. His parents may not have been seers. Badyaranké are not bothered by this inconsistency.

## CHAPTER FIVE

*Internal Powers:*
*The Witch*

## THE ATTRIBUTES OF WITCHES

If the Badyaranké do not give careful attention to village and compound rites, consult frequently with marabouts, and avoid contact with polluting creatures, these people believe that sicknesses, accidents, and deaths will occur even more frequently than they do. The Badyaranké believe that most misfortune is the unavoidable consequence of human collision with the nocturnal world. Most sicknesses, accidents, and deaths — I was told repeatedly — are caused by witches.

Within the seer category exists a division between those people who use their power to kill and those who do not. The latter group is referred to as seers (umadisé), while the killers are known as witches — in Badyaranké, *ngontunné,* an ugly, frightening, and whispered word. A witch reportedly captures and eats his prey's soul by unknowable means that cannot be viewed through ordinary human eyes. The Badyaranké believe that after a witch has killed an individual, he invites his colleagues — other witches who generally live in his village but who may come from other villages and tribes — to join him in devouring the soul. By attending the feast, each guest acquires an obligation to return the favor to his host whenever he wishes to collect this "credit." Debts proliferate with each kill, and thus the threat of killings by witches never abates. Within the system of soul reciprocity, anyone may give and receive credit: parents may give credit to children, husbands to wives, and Badyaranké to strangers.

A witch who has served as host, it is said, will eventually arrive in the village of his debtor to announce his impatience for a soul. If the creditor is a Badyaranké, he appears as a bird (known as comidyidyi) who cries like a large owl. Seers supposedly have the ability to distinguish between the call of a real owl and the ominous signal of a transformed witch. The musket fired during my second night at Tonghia (see Chapter 1) was directed at a large owl who apparently grunted from a housetop that it wanted an old favor to be returned; it flew out of the compound into the forest so hurriedly, it was said, that no misfortune resulted from his visit. My young assistant once told me: "He [comidyidyi] is like a bird — head, wings, and feet. He goes into a hen house and takes a chicken's head and wears it. There is a story of a man who traded heads with a chicken at night but didn't come back early enough in the morning, and the chicken ran away and kept his head." If the creditor is a Fula Kunda, villagers say he cries like a small owl (cowaeo). If the debtor is unable to procure a soul, he risks losing his own soul to appease his once generous host.

The Badyaranké believe that witches, like seers, can transform themselves freely into a monkey, snake, anthill, tree, breeze — almost anything. One particular type of witch (difuta) is identifiable by non-seers because of a red light which beams from time to time from his or her anus. The light is said to be harmless, and as unconscious as a smile. An elder said he once saw red lights coming from the anus of an adult woman whose young daughter he wished to marry. Although this happened long ago

97

and details were confused and forgotten, the elder did recall he failed in his attempt to secure the daughter's hand in marriage despite his threat to expose the mother's secret.

A witch is said to possess a name "of the night"[1] known only to other witches, and to kill with guns, ropes, clubs, knives, and poisons of the night — in one instance by suspending a victim (one of my neighbors) over a river of the night.[2] All artifacts of the night can be seen by seers and witches, and by them alone. For example, if an enterprising witch were to build a snare of the night along the path, a non-seer would walk through it unaware and probably uninjured, non-seers being harder to kill.

The witches of a particular village are organized, having their own chief, musicians who honor him, and subjects. Just as the village chief is the highest political functionary in Badyaranké society, the witches recognize no leader beyond the village level. (Among the Fula Kunda, who at one time were organized into supra-village political units, there are witch chiefs who also administer many villages.) Status among witches is earned, just as it is among ordinary people. To become a chief among witches, it is said a witch must kill a newly circumcised boy and offer his soul for common consumption — a difficult feat because the circumcised boys are guarded by reputable seers.

Anyone can be a witch. Formerly witches were said to be old people, but now, I was told, everyone is doing it, with the exception of boys and girls under circumcision and excision ages, who are not yet "strong" enough to exercise their power. A male informant said that if an old woman is a seer, then probably she is a witch, and elderly female witches, in addition to being numerous, are also very powerful. Blacksmiths, although known to be seers, are seldom thought to be witches because if a smith eats a soul he no longer can work iron, and his tools will shatter for everyone to see — even if he wishes to kill he cannot do so without revealing himself. Elderly retired hunters frequently engage in

[1] Existing only in the realm of witchcraft.
[2] See Case 5, page 122.

witchcraft, so one young man told me, because they have long cultivated a taste for meat.

Witches need no other motive for their deeds than to eat and to repay their debts to each other. The choice of particular victims, however, is determined by two independent factors: a witch kills someone who is easy for him to obtain and by whose death he risks small threat of reprisal; secondly, a witch kills those for whom he has anger (*kangfa*). But these two factors only help explain why some victims are chosen, not why witches kill. The reason behind killings is unrelated to facility or to sentiment; witches kill to eat and to fulfill obligations between themselves. The situation as the Badyaranké conceive it differs from Max Gluckman's observation, derived from E. E. Evans-Pritchard's research among the Azande, that bad feeling sets the power to work.[3] Anger may guide the witch's choice, but his drive is inherent and goaded by debts to his peers.

Several conversations with my assistant and with two other adult men revealed some of the factors they expected witches would consider when selecting their victims. The matrisib nephew or niece (nimé) is said to be the "easiest" relative to obtain as a victim because blood relatives would be less likely to seek vengeance. Killing a son involves more risk since he is not of the father's sib, and the son's sib relatives might choose to redress their loss. A male witch would not care to kill his wife because it would be costly and difficult to replace her. A female witch might, however, appropriate her husband, perhaps to dissolve her connection to an unfriendly co-wife. In-laws who are too demanding would also be favored prey. Witches generally choose victims from among their village neighbors and would not take the life of someone from another tribe, although the exchange of souls may cross tribal boundaries. Witches tend to kill other seers because they can recognize each other and because the seer's soul may be caught on a voyage.

Although witches do not cause plagues, they can profit from

---

[3] Gluckman 1963:82.

them and help spread them. For example, if Tonghia suffers from a plague, a witch from a nearby village could lead one of his neighbors there and kill him, making it appear as though he died of plague. A chief of the witches in Tonghia might give some of the plague to the witches of the other community. When many people suffer from disease, the witches have a free hand to kill since blame is difficult to pin down; ordinarily, however, witches abstain from collective murder. The Badyaranké never fear eating with a crowd of people because no witch would poison a group for fear of killing an unintended victim; conversely, they think it is always dangerous to eat alone.

Certain places and times are considered to be fraught with more danger from witchcraft than others. The village is more dangerous than the bush "because they [witches] are of the village. It is here that people are always together." But the bush is not immune, for "the places chosen for attack depend on the habits of the chosen victim, where he goes." Midday and midnight are the most critical hours. Night is more dangerous than day because everyone can readily be found in his house. Likewise, midday is more dangerous than morning or afternoon; since it is hotter, everyone is in the village eating or napping. The long dry season is dangerous because it is hot, and the rainy season is dangerous because it is dark. But the cold dry period during the rice harvest, when all the young men are away, is the worst time of the year. Then the village is quiet and partially abandoned; its strong young men are gone. "The witches come to eat the new rice and its owner. They don't like to eat newly harvested rice without the meat of a person." The most feared place of all is the village center at night during the period of the rice harvest. This same location where people sit, laugh, and gossip during the day becomes the most dreaded area, abandoned after nightfall. A monster, reputed to be an old female witch of the village, is said to roam the center at night, stomping the earth like a horse and breathing fire. At least four young men of Tonghia have encountered this creature on their midnight journeys to their girlfriends' compounds. One man who was hiking alone during this time of the year reported that he saw a house move ahead of him into the road, pause, then wander into the forest. Though he did not know *who* the house was, he was certain that it was *someone*, rather than something.

The powers of the witch, as well as the seer, are said to be transmitted from one generation to the next through heredity. If the father or the mother is a witch and the child is born a seer, the parent may try to persuade the child to participate in the witches' feasts. "If a man is a witch, he chooses the child he likes best to become a witch, and the favorite usually consents to learn. If a child refuses to learn, the father tries to kill him." Likewise, if a mother tries to tempt her seer child to eat a soul with her and the child refuses, this rejection will spoil their relationship. (Such a refusal was said to have happened in one case known to me, but I never learned of any indications that the mother and her son were on bad terms.) If a woman is a witch and eats a soul while pregnant, the child is also said to eat, though involuntarily, and to become a witch. For him there is no choice.

IDENTIFICATION OF WITCHES

The essential fact about a witch is that his appearance is no different from anyone else's. The Badyaranké say that reliable knowledge about witches comes only from seers, marabouts, and a number of oracular techniques. Unlike the Azande [4] or the Tiv,[5] the Badyaranké do not need to perform an autopsy to identify a witch, because the organ of witchcraft, the eyes of the night, can be seen by seers. A marabout is frequently consulted after a death or in event of sickness to divine, by dreaming or other methods, the cause of the misfortune. To obtain divination through a dream, the client visits the marabout in his house in the evening and explains his question. The marabout listens, recites a verse over his prayer beads, places an amulet under his bed, and goes to sleep. In the morning, he relates his dream for a small fee of 10–100 francs (4–40 cents); the dream may reveal a

[4] Evans-Pritchard 1937:40.
[5] L. Bohannan 1958:59–61; L. Bohannan and P. Bohannan 1953:84–85; P. Bohannan 1958:3–4.

description of a witch — whether he is young or old, male or female, dark or light — and tell where he lives but it is said not to provide his name.

In Portuguese Guinea live two Manding marabouts, Lawalli and Sekuna, said to be brothers, who are the most important diviners for the whole eastern region of the Casamance, northwestern Guinea, and northeastern Portuguese Guinea. Unfortunately, I was never able to interview them. Lawalli and his brother are the only marabouts who satisfy people's appetite for specific accusations by naming the witches. (An old man at Tonghia said that before Lawalli, the people could not learn witches' names from marabouts.) The brothers reportedly read the name from the Koran, see the individual in a special mirror, or play a drum that makes witches run to them and confess.

Lawalli and Sekuna travel widely during the dry season, a time when the villagers are still solvent from their peanut sales. The brothers provide answers for all possible questions at the rate of 300 francs ($1.20) apiece. When they identify a witch, they call for him to have his eyes of the night removed. This they do by making a small incision under each of his eyes, charging him the punishing fee of 5,000 francs ($20).

Everyone thinks the brothers' rates are outrageous, but most believe in the infallibility of their decisions. However, one civil servant once said that Lawalli is a fraud because he has "something hidden in his drum that makes witches confess." A medic in a distant village told me that he knew of Lawalli's powers but would only believe in them when Lawalli resuscitates a witch's victim. These are the most skeptical remarks on the powers of the two brothers that I was able to collect.

How the brothers learn names and diagnose situations is unknown. Perhaps they keep informed about events in their territory and even have some system of informants. When they travel from one village to another, they do bring porters from the last village to accompany them to the next. During this time they could gather information about the next stop, although the Tonghia people deny that they ask such questions. The only divinations I witnessed were done by unknown marabouts, early in my fieldwork, so I never learned firsthand what the brothers did or said. My closest contact with Lawalli came while visiting a small market town where he was temporarily in residence, but he was unavailable for interview because he was living in the house of the Prefect and absorbed in official business.

In addition to the visions of seers and marabouts, the Badyaranké know at least six oracular techniques for obtaining information about witches. Two of these, the contractual shrine (koasé) and the hammock oracle, have been described in Chapters 3 and 4. The others are freely translated as the iron oracle, poison oracle, cock testicles oracle, and anvil oracle, and are outlined below.

If a person is accused of killing by witchcraft or of having participated in a soul feast, the accused may vindicate himself by asking the blacksmith to heat a piece of iron until it is red and and then to place it in a nest of leaves held in his cupped hands. The individual who refuses to take the hot iron test, or whose hands are burned by it is assumed guilty.

The Badyaranké formerly practiced a form of poison oracle, using a powdered bark of a tree found in the Guinea forest far to the south. This bark would be mixed with water and was said to have the power to kill the witch or sicken the seer who drank it. The witch would vomit, urinate, admit all of his crimes, and probably die.

Anyone can learn through the cock testicles oracle if a deceased person has been the victim of witchcraft. A cock is taken to the grave or to a fork in the path, and the investigator says, "If X died a natural death, let the testicles be white, and if he died by witchcraft, let them be black." He then cuts the chicken open for inspection. This method can only demonstrate presence or absence of witchcraft; more detailed clues must come from the contractual shrine, the marabout, or a seer.

The final technique, the anvil oracle, resembles the koasé and consists of a miniature iron anvil that can be owned by anyone. My informants knew of one in Coniagui country near Youkounkoun in Guinea and one at Kutan; once an old woman of Tonghia owned one, but she has since died and the technique was abandoned. If someone dies and a second individual has reason to accuse a third of witchcraft, they may appeal to the anvil by giving a chicken to the owner. He kills it and says "If the accusation is justified, let the accused die in three years." If the accused does die within three years, his clothing must be brought to the owner as proof of his guilt. If relatives of the accused wear the clothing before notifying the owner, they too may die.

Witchcraft may be suspected, but never brought into the open. Or the suspicions may become common knowledge, but remain a private affair. Or the accusation may be vented in public, quite probably cause a fight, and require a meeting of elders. If the incident is serious and convincing, an entire village has been known to tie and beat a witch. Villagers say that convicted witches were previously killed and abandoned where they died, without proper dignity of burial. No one knows precisely how witches were killed, and no elder remembers a single death not followed by burial, which leads to the suspicion that no witch was ever actually killed. The most powerful sanction, other than execution, is to drive the witch from the village. Witches may spar between themselves, but public revenge against witches takes the form of beating, contracts with shrines, and sorcery.

Protection against witchcraft encompasses many items described in Chapter 3 — Koranic and pagan amulets, offerings prescribed by a marabout, Koranic waters, and the leaves, roots, and petals of a wild bush (*dioutou*). (Branches of this bush are placed beside, over, or beneath doorways to protect a dwelling from witches.) Another method is employed by women who have borne children who died in infancy. To make a child less appealing to a witch who might wish to take him away, a woman may temporarily give her child an unattractive name (perhaps an equivalent to *feces* or *no-name*). Anyone recording Badyaranké genealogies will encounter some surprising names as a result of this usage.

A WITCHCRAFT TALE

Mamadou, the seer described in Chapter 4, knew a great many tales about animals, spirits, and people. One evening in my little round house, he recited the following tale of witchcraft — the only one I collected. Actual accounts of witches are so fascinating that they need not be improved upon by the storyteller's imagination. While the tale was being delivered, in Badyaranké, I transcribed it in this fairly free translation, with my assistant's help:

There was a village where every inhabitant was a witch — men, women, and children — and they ate every baby. In this village of witches was a woman and her mother. One day the daughter had a child, a girl. The grandmother took the girl to another village where there were no witches. The girl stayed there until marriageable age; then she married and had a child. The second time there was a child in her stomach, he said, "I want to be born." The mother said, "If a child can talk like that, he can deliver himself." The child said, "All right, I'll deliver myself," and he came out her finger tip. He said to his mother, "You must give me a name." She said, "If you are capable of delivering yourself, you can give yourself a name." The child said, "Good, I christen myself! I call myself Yamburss."

After a while, the second child began to walk. His mother said to her husband, I must go to see my mother and my father because I don't know them." The second child said, "I want to go." The mother said, "No," and they argued. The next morning the first child, the mother, and the husband took the road to visit her mother and father in the village of witches. The child who came out the finger followed them. The mother beat him; he returned to the village but came back again. He was beaten a second time and went back to the village. Since the child was chased twice, he did not want to take the road. He went very far in the brush and then came out on the road. His mother wanted to send him back, but the husband said, "Let him come; it's too far to go back." The mother asked, "Can you walk?" The child said, "Yes," and they went on.

Along the road they found a field full of rice where the cultivators were walking on their hands and working with their feet. The child sang, "Where is the village of Cumbasse Maré [the grandmother]?" The cultivators showed them the road, and they continued. They found women who were washing in the river; they were standing on their hands and washing with their feet. The child sang again, "Where is the village of Cumbasse Maré, Cumbasse Maré who kills people to eat?" After the women showed them the route, they continued. Next they met some people who walked with their hands and carried calabashes with their feet. The child sang the same song. The people said to the child, "There is Cumbasse Maré who winnows with her ears." The ears of the grandmother whistled in the wind making a great noise. They went to the grandmother who was working with her ears. The child sang again, "Where is the village of Cumbasse Maré, Cumbasse

Maré who kills people to eat?" The grandmother did not hear anything because her ears were whistling. The child sang again. There was another woman nearby who heard; she took the ears of the grandmother and said, "Someone is calling you, and you don't hear." They went on; the grandmother took the baggage and led them to her house. There they were greeted and were content.

In the village, the grandmother had taken much credit, and she was pleased that her relatives had come. She went to the village and said, "There, my relatives have come; I will repay you all. This evening I will put human flesh in their meal, and when they eat it, they will die." The smallest child warned, "The old woman will bring some rice but don't eat it, even if I'm not here. If we eat that, we will all die." He was seated near the door; the grandmother brought the rice to the house, but the small boy at the door did not see that someone had brought rice. The mother, father, and older child ate the rice; when they ate, their stomachs became swollen. The child saw that his kin had swollen stomachs. He asked, "Why did you eat the rice?" The mother replied, "Why not? If someone brings rice it's to be eaten." The boy said, "You shouldn't have eaten. If I wasn't with you, you would all die." That evening the grandmother brought rice with fonio and put human flesh in the rice, but not in the fonio. The child said, "Leave the rice and eat the fonio." The grandmother said, "Why don't you want to eat the rice?" The child said, "Because we don't know fonio — where we live they don't grow it — we want to taste the fonio."

That evening they were asleep. The grandmother came to the door and said, "With this sword I will kill the children who sleep here." The little boy did not sleep, but the others did. The boy said, "We aren't sleeping yet." The grandmother asked why. The boy said, "Because there are too many lice in the bed." The grandmother went to get blankets for them and said, "Put that on the bed." The grandmother came again and said, "With this knife I will kill the children who sleep." The child said, "We are not sleeping." She asked why again. He said, "Because there are too many mosquitoes." The old woman went to get a mosquito net and said, "Arrange that." After the grandmother brought the mosquito net, the child made a hole in the house to go very far away. He defecated at the door of the house. When the grandmother returned, she said, "With this knife I will kill the children." The feces said, "We are not sleeping." The child with his mother, father, and brother escaped through the hole; he took two eggs and a palm nut with him. The grandmother came back, but the door was always closed. She said, "They sleep." The cock sang three times, and day had come. The grandmother asked, "Why do you sleep like that until morning? I will wake you up." When she entered, she stepped in the feces, right up to her chest. She looked in the bed and there was no one. She thought and thought, and then went to wash.

She came back again, found the hole, and entered. She ran and ran until ten in the morning; she saw the child far away and cried, "Stop!" The child replied, "We are here." She said, "Wait for me." The child answered, "You come here." When the grandmother was close, the child broke the eggs on the ground and they made a great sea. The grandmother stood at the edge of the sea. Since she was a witch, she tapped her thigh and out came one thousand people; she tapped the other and out came one thousand gourds. They threw all the water out of the way, and the grandmother passed.

She followed them again and found them ahead, about to leave the hole. The old woman said, "Wait for me." The child replied, "Come here. We're here." When the old woman was near, the child said to his parents, "Come close to me." He tapped the palm nut on the ground; it became a very high tree, and they climbed it. The grand-mother came with four sacks. The child said, "When she comes, don't look down." The old woman said to the child, "You think that I can't catch you." The child said, "In any case we are there." The old woman took the sack and said, "*Cum ba dungel mama dungel* [magic words]." The mother said, "I'm tired," and she fell into the sack. The grandmother tied it and opened another sack. She repeated the same words; the father said, "I'm tired," and also fell. The grandmother fastened the sack and took another. The brother also fell; only the youngest was left. The grandmother tried to make the child fall but could not, so she climbed up the tree herself. When she arrived half-way, the child transformed himself into a lizard. He descended and released his mother, father, and brother, and said the magic words to the grandmother. She looked down and fell into the sack. The child fastened it and said to his father and brother, "Let's cut some wood to make a big fire." They cut the wood, made a big fire, and threw in the sack with the grandmother inside.

When it was all burned, the child took the lower jawbone. He said to his parents, "Let's go, but I'm not going back. I will go into busi-ness." He told his parents to go, and they separated. [The remainder of Mamadou's story tells how the child met a panther, hyena, lion, and wild dog who had a herd of cows, and of how, through a series of clever tricks, aided by his grandmother's jaw, he managed to acquire their herd for himself, and returned with it to his parents.]

SUMMARY

According to Badyaranké theory, witches know and have reasons for what they do, and to this extent they are definitely conscious agents. However, in my own experience, no suspected witch was aware of the evil that he was thought to have done before being accused.

Both Clyde Kluckhohn and John Middleton wrote of beliefs similar to Badyaranké (to the extent that individual physical suffering is blamed upon other humans who may or may not have inherent powers, who act upon their victim by mystical rather than physical means) held by the Navaho of the American Southwest and the Lugbara of western Uganda, respectively. Kluckhohn and Middleton attributed constructive functions to such seemingly antisocial beliefs. They observed that witches provide a mirror image, a kind of absolute negative standard, against which the morally upright citizen may be compared.[6] Similar functions were attributed by E. H. Winter to comparable witchcraft beliefs held by the Amba who live on the Uganda-Congo border. Speaking specifically of the relation between beliefs about mystical evildoers and the social order among the Amba, Winter wrote, "There is a formal congruence between the set of ideas and the social structure . . . the ideas which the Amba hold about witches are not random . . . they are exact inversions of the social order." [7]

The inverse relationship between witchcraft beliefs and social structure seen among the Navaho, Lugbara, and Amba is also in evidence among the Badyaranké. In terms of moral and physical attributes, witches among the Badyaranké are invisible, live by night, turn into animals, winnow with their ears, walk upside down, cause families to break up, and follow overriding imperatives to kill. Unlike the sprites who engage in mutually profitable conversions between the visible world and the world of the night, witches appropriate the souls (by killing people) for use among themselves, and make no return at all. Men and women work to create and sustain life; witches work to release it, to exploit the hard-won social and cultural order for their own ends. The fickle visitation of sickness and death—believed to be caused by witches — is considered to be tangible proof of the potential

[6] Kluckhohn 1962:110; Middleton 1963:271.
[7] 1963:299.

frailty of the most intimate ties between people. Any relationships, however close, may be sacrificed when the comidyidyi appears with an urgent message. Thus, witches are "inverted" [8] and an abhorrent reminder of "primordial slime." [9] This means essentially that witches contradict people's notions of how the world should be — and how people should act. They defy physical constraints, they contradict basic categories (i.e., they may mix together parts of birds, monkeys, and men, or they mix different domains of existence, such as being a person and being a kettle or wind at the same time), and they act in ways that men should not act. This worst kind of evildoer is represented as the ultimate "abomination" [10] in a reasonably well-ordered world. Lucy Mair, in an effort to understand why similar images of witches are found in different parts of the world, speculated that since "the way witches behave . . . is . . . the antithesis of good. And since the elementary requirements of social order are everywhere the same, one should expect that there would be more resemblances than differences in different people's imaginary pictures of the witch." [11]

However, the Badyaranké witches (and possibly those of the Lugbara and Amba) would probably object to being reduced to what E. H. Winter describes as "exact inversions of the social order," [12] for they participate in an elaborate social network that closely resembles, in structure if not content, that of humans, and operates according to the eminently social principles of obligation and reciprocity. Even sanctions exist for those witches who have failed to contribute their share of souls, which are furnished in much the same fashion as are the products of female labor in the compound — one witch prepares today, and another tomorrow, until all have had their turn.

---

[8] Middleton 1963:271.
[9] Turner 1964:323.
[10] *Abomination* is used here in the same sense that it is used in Chapter 3 of Mary Douglas's *Purity and Danger*, entitled "The Abominations of Leviticus," pp. 41–57.
[11] 1969:38.
[12] 1963:299.

## CHAPTER SIX

# Some Case Studies
# of Misfortune

## INTRODUCTION

This chapter contains a number of case studies of misfortunes
and their interpretations, which have been gleaned from interviews and, whenever practical, from first-hand observation. In
each case, as much background detail as possible was collected
in order to investigate the manner in which particular explanations were attributed to particular events. The process by which
the Badyaranké arrive at an interpretation seems to involve a mysterious emergence of a consensus, or a narrowing of alternatives,
in the minds of those concerned.

At least three levels of causation may pertain to any one misfortune. At the most specific level, people are burned- by fire, bitten by snakes, and sickened by disease. At the most abstract level,
all that takes place on earth is permitted by Kodan who is the
source of order, and the ultimate giver and taker of life and
fortune. Between these two levels, being witnessed by Kodan and

making use of the countless specific empirical expedients, the spirit beings are responsible for a particular misfortune befalling a particular individual. Through the spirits, events in the observable world of experience acquire meaning; the spirits answer the questions, "Why did this happen to me?" and "Why did this happen to him?" The spirit causes of adult sickness and accidents stem from witchcraft, sorcery, genies, and sprites; in addition, the causes for child sickness include pollution taboos and ancestors.

Cases of misfortune, especially those that involve suspicions of witchcraft, have been chosen for analysis for a variety of reasons. First, the Badyaranké are more likely to seek an explanation for a misfortune, and these explanations tend to be remembered. Secondly, misfortunes provide a convenient means of viewing the relationships between the spirits and the events that they are believed to control. Good fortune, in the sense of absence of bad fortune, is not a matter for extensive or urgent speculation.[1] Finally, the selection of seers and witches as the focus of study reflects certain of my own interests, but these interests are shared by the Badyaranké. As much as possible, the general field of misfortune is covered, and not simply those cases that produced accusations of witchcraft and sorcery; for, as Daryll Forde demonstrated in his chapter entitled "Spirits, Witches, and Sorcerers"[2] about the supernatural economy of the Yakö, it may be as revealing to observe when witchcraft is not invoked as an explanation as when it is. Only through an appreciation of the alternatives available within the culture can an understanding be gained of the covert logic which underlies their selective penetration into actual affairs. Kluckhohn remarked in *Navaho Witchcraft*:

It is worth noting that man not only craves reasons and explanations, but in most cases these reasons involve some form of personification,

---

[1] Excesses of good fortune, however, may be causally linked to suffering when they are explained in the idiom of seers, genies, and sprites. This association of good fortune and suffering is reflected in the interpretations Badyaranké give to certain dreams: if one dreams of a funeral in a compound, it means that a feast will take place there, and conversely, if one dreams of feasting, it means that misfortune is not far away.

[2] 1964:210–233.

some human-like agency either natural or supernatural. It seems that only a small minority among highly sophisticated peoples can fairly face impersonal forces and the phenomena of chance.[3]

The Badyaranké explain their suffering in terms of "human-like" agencies, but they also explain their suffering in terms of "impersonal forces" and sometimes they simply let the matter lie. These last two alternatives allow respite in an otherwise closed system where personal suffering suggests personal causes and leads very easily to blame.

Presentation of the data through a series of case studies conveys an appearance of objectivity and is even considered to be a method of analysis by some. In these studies of instances of misfortune, especially when they involved accusations of witchcraft, I could never get the story straight; for individual loyalties, hatreds, and disinterest yielded many different versions of the same incident. Beyond a few fixed demographic, vital, and sociological details, most cases became a quagmire of inconsistencies that deepened, rather than firmed, with additional research. Inconsistency per se should not be considered a limitation or weakness of the material, because although a researcher might elicit a precise genealogy or record a complete census, the actions of witches and spirits and their interactions with men reflect situational judgments and volatile points of view. Accuracy in such cases may be expressed in the uncertainty of the several versions, which in most cases cannot be reduced to an unambiguous account and cannot be provided by a single informant, however gifted or detached he might be. Some of these cases border on myth, and others include as much cultural and sociological information as was possible to discover.

CASE 1: WITCHCRAFT AND THE
FOUNDING OF TONGHIA

At the village of Timbi in Guinea lived a woman who had killed her own unmarried daughter and had given parts of the soul to

3 Kluckhohn 1962:107.

several people on credit. When the pioneers left Timbi to found Tonghia, this woman notified her debtors that she wished to be repaid. Waliouae, the new chief of Tonghia, asked her to wait until the village was established, and not to spoil the village before it even began. She persisted, however, but was finally driven away and told never to return. During the first year at Tonghia there was a drought, and the stream that passes by the village began to dry up. During that same year, the daughter and sister's son of Waliouae died unexpectedly, and eventually the water returned.

The elders claim that the death of the children and the return of the water are related events, although no one knows exactly what happened. Three of the original settlers said that Waliouae was supposed to have been a seer and that he made a pact in his house one night with the genies of the stream. This was no usual contract, however; for although he is said to have promised two human lives (that were easy for him to take) for the return of the water, the lives were thought to have been taken by certain unknown witches of the village, who did the unpleasant task for the chief.

These early incidents are mentioned because the founding of a village is thought to be a critical time. An old blacksmith once said that smiths avoid participating in the founding of a village since someone important must be sacrificed during the early months of settlement; because of their estimate of the importance of their powers, they fear for their own safety. The villagers talk of the deaths of the two children as if they were actually sacrificed, but from the known circumstances, they appear to have died from premature but natural causes at a time that corresponded with an increase in water. (I suspect that everything that happened during the first year of settlement was scrutinized for its meaning.) Although the losses of a person's own child and a sister's son could be construed as evidence that the person is a dangerous witch, in this case the old chief emerged from the situation as a benefactor in the villagers' eyes, more admired than ever.

After Waliouae's death, his compound was under the headmanship of his sister's son, Kelifa, and after Kelifa's death, Waliba
succeeded as headman. Waliba too was a sister's son of Waliouae,
of the matrisib Binyassi. At the time in question, some twenty
years ago, the male members of the compound included Waliba,
his inherited son Abdullae, Boumbali Nkèta, Niaboli Culoni,
Bandia Cumpa, Kamara Tamba, and Niaboli Diandian. Niaboli
Culoni was next to Waliba in authority because he was the leader
of the younger working men; as a son of the deceased Waliouae,
he was also a son of Waliba.

Waliba's son Abdullae said the reason that Waliba and Culoni
separated was because Waliba does not appreciate those who
work for him. The two men were generally on good terms, and
Culoni even refused an opportunity for marriage out of loyalty
to Waliba; the girl's parents had asked Culoni to move to their
compound as a condition of marriage, which he refused, thereby
forfeiting the girl. At that time, all the men worked one collective field and rotated to work in each other's private fields. Culoni,
Abdullae said, was obedient to Waliba, and they quarrelled little
about work.

Then Culoni, who had a joint field with Waliba, got married
and decided to clear his own cash-crop peanut field. He became
an independent family head within the compound and began
earning as much as Waliba on his sales. Waliba, who is a proud
cultivator, was annoyed. The two senior men drifted farther and
farther apart; Waliba confided fewer of his plans to Culoni. In a
separate incident, Bandia Cumpa was struck by Waliba during
an argument concerning work in the collective field, and considered the humiliation to have been unwarranted. Culoni began
to eat apart with Cumpa, Tamba, and Diandian, leaving Waliba
with Abdullae and Boumbali Nkèta.

Waliba's first and favorite wife Sanumu died, and this event
kindled the disintegration of the compound. Although Abdullae explained the separation in terms of Waliba's insensitivity to

the wishes of his followers, several others in the village, including Waliba, explained the whole affair in terms of witchcraft. The following account is pieced together from discussions with Waliba, Cumpa, and a third man. I was advised not to discuss the matter with Culoni, the suspected witch, so I never did.

One afternoon the wife of Tamba was walking to the fields, and on the path she saw something nightmarish. She returned to the village and said that never again would she go alone to the fields. She had seen something that she could describe to no one. It was a witch, waiting to kill someone. Two days later, Sanumu, Waliba's wife, was preparing to go to the fields around midday to collect some bundles of millet. Waliba cautioned her to go later because the sun was high overhead, but she refused, saying that she had other work to do later in the rice gardens. Culoni waited for her on the path, and at the same place where the other woman was frightened, Culoni fired his "gun of the night" and hit her on the back of the neck. She returned to the village and said she was sick. Water was coming out of the spot where the ball had struck. Waliba said that the next day he would consult a marabout, but the next day she died. She did not identify the killer, but a marabout was said to have suggested Culoni. Waliba explained it thus: "To be together, you must dispute and argue. One doesn't leave a compound because of arguments; they're part of living. No one proved Culoni did it. No one saw him do it. It was a forgotten marabout, some twenty years ago. The marabout said the killer was in the compound, and since people were suspecting Culoni, that's how it was." Waliba knew of no motive for such an act and claimed that there had been no enmity between Culoni and his dead wife.

Waliba went north to the town of Tambacounda and plotted with a marabout to kill Culoni by sorcery. Culoni is said to have sought another marabout who told him to defend himself by burying one hundred pebbles under his rear door. The force sent by Waliba arrived one night but found Culoni safely enclosed, as if in an iron fortress. Waliba consulted a second marabout who said that he could do nothing against Culoni, as did a third. Waliba abandoned his efforts, but because of the hard feeling caused by the accusations, Culoni moved out of the compound. He created a new compound next to Waliba's and brought with him Tamba, Diandian, Cumpa, and (the following year) Boumbali Nkèta. Waliba was left with his son and two wives. Culoni and his followers cleared their own collective field, and the separation was complete.

The ill feeling between Waliba and Culoni apparently originated in Waliba's unwillingness to accept Culoni's increasing autonomy. It is inconceivable that such an issue could be brought before the council of elders for discussion and eventual resolution. The death of Waliba's wife was a severe loss to him and probably would have required an explanation, even if the compound was not divided into uneasy factions. The timing of her death, however, gave Waliba the opportunity to express his jealousy and dissatisfaction. Suspicion and rumor were sufficient for him to accuse Culoni, even though his guilt was never tested, admitted, or proven.

The motivating relationship in this case is not between the witch and victim, but rather between the witch and his accuser; for Culoni's motive in attacking the woman was only relevant because she was Waliba's wife. Although it might be argued that this case pinpoints a structural tension between father and son in a matrilineal society, the fission itself displayed no clear pattern in kinship relationships. Waliba remained with his one inherited son, and Culoni left with one man from his own matrisib and three others from Waliba's matrisib, who were as Waliba was, his terminological fathers. Now that Waliba and Culoni have been living apart for many years, their hard feelings have cooled, and Waliba is apparently less certain that witchcraft was involved. Cumpa, who is now on bad terms with Culoni, has no doubt that Culoni did the deed. Abdullae, who is unhappy in Waliba's compound and who has already withdrawn from collective labors, explains the incident entirely in terms of Waliba's injustices. Others in the village who like to gossip but who had no direct connection to the case perpetuate the belief that Culoni is a very powerful witch, for such accusations are never forgotten.

Kamara Tamba, a sister's son of Waliba, was one of those who left with Culoni to found the new compound. He, with his full brother Niambi, and Diandian then moved to another compound, next moved back with Waliba, then back with Culoni. Tamba, like Waliba, is a terminological father of Culoni although, unlike Waliba, he is slightly younger than Culoni; Diandian is a sister's son of Culoni and thus, like Culoni, a son of Tamba.

Tamba had married five women who were either widows to whom he had no claim, or whose bridewealth had been begun by other men. Three of these women died young, and a fourth died unexpectedly during childbirth, while Tamba was residing in Culoni's compound. Not long after the death of his fourth wife, Tamba was hunting in the forest and was hit in the chest by a bullet fired by his neighbor Adion. Adion said he had fired at a small antelope, and the ball struck Tamba but did not penetrate his flesh. Adion, Tamba's equal in years, is also a member of his matrisib — Binyassi. Someone, Tamba said, caused that bullet to find him to spoil relations between him and his neighbor and kinsman. A marabout told Tamba that a witch had led the bullet to him, and if he did not leave Tonghia that very year, he would either die or be helplessly sick; the marabout also said that a man and a woman were conspiring against him. Tamba said he feared that he had many enemies because of his easily-come-by wives, but did not know which ones in particular were after him. According to Cumpa, Tamba was once more certain of Culoni's involvement in his misfortunes, although Tamba denied this.

Diandian's son was then bitten by a poisonous snake and became painfully ill, but did not die. Diandian learned from a marabout that the serpent was someone in his own compound, and if he did not take care, he would lose his son. Then Diandian became ill and feared dying, so he moved to the Fula Kunda village of Akan to convalesce. Diandian made public accusations that Culoni, his mother's brother, was trying to eat his soul. Seven years ago Tamba, his brother Niambi, and Diandian left

Tonghia to construct a new compound in the Peul Fouta village of Chafen. Although they told Culoni they were going for only one year, they remained there until 1968. Tamba said that he was not happy to leave Tonghia, but considers himself safer in his own compound.

This case is significant because there seemed not to be prior conflicts in social relations between either of the accusers and Culoni, the accused. Both Tamba and Diandian suspected witchcraft because of the sheer burden of their misfortunes; Tamba harbored some anxieties about the ways in which he acquired his wives, but these ways did not involve Culoni. Perhaps because of the stigma acquired from Waliba's suspicions, Culoni was suspected this second time, although again, his guilt was never admitted or proven. As in the dissolution of Waliba's compound, no clear pattern can be discerned in who left and who remained. Tamba left with Niambi his full brother, Masse who is a father to Tamba as Tamba is a father to Culoni, and Diandian who, like Culoni, is Tamba's son.

CASE 4: KUFÉ AND THE ANTELOPE

Kufé was a friend of Waliba's inherited son Abdullae. Since Waliba's compound was underpopulated after the departures of Culoni and his followers, Kufé was asked by Abdullae to move to the compound with his young wife and two young children. Kufé came principally because he was a friend of Waliba's son; in addition, Waliba is a grandfather of Kufé, and Waliba's third wife, Koba, was a wife-giver to Kufé. Koba belongs to the same matrisib as the father of Kufé's wife. Koba is a known witch whose most celebrated evil deed was to help kill the father of Kufé's wife.

While Kufé was living in the compound, it was rumored that he had committed adultery with one of Abdullae's wives, and the two men became estranged. Kufé said that he tried on several occasions to persuade Abdullae of the falsity of the rumors. But eventually Abdullae stopped speaking to Kufé, his dislike for Kufé became common knowledge, and Kufé felt unwelcome in his new compound. The two men never fought, and hostility between them was not severe enough to warrant the laborious and dramatic act of moving out. Kufé stubbornly maintains his innocence and claims to have wished for an eventual reconciliation.

When Kufé moved to Waliba's compound, he had two young children, a boy and a girl. After his second child, the girl, was born, he and his wife made a sacrifice to the nightjar and subsequently paid with two chickens. Kufé claims to have broken the eggs of the bird, and made his payment because the children were both living. A third child was born while they were residing in Waliba's compound, and died two years later. Then their girl fell sick. Kufé sent two trusted friends (a young man of his matrisib and a young man who was paying bridewealth for a girl of Kufé's matrisib) to consult Lawalli the marabout, who said that the girl had eaten poison on the day of a work party in Kufé's peanut field. Kufé had been ill himself that day, and gave Waliba a goat to feed the men who worked for him. Lawalli said the girl had eaten poison that had been given by an unidentified Fula Kunda. Despite the marabout's advice, and despite the evidence of previous mystical contamination from the nightjar, Kufé was certain that Waliba's wife, Koba, was to blame.

He moved back to the compound from which he had come, after four years with Waliba and Abdullae. One week after he moved, his ailing daughter died. He subsequently consulted two Fula Kunda marabouts who both confirmed that the girl had been poisoned on the day of the work party and that a dark old woman was responsible, thus confirming Kufé's suspicion of Koba, who fits this description. Kufé said he left Waliba's compound because of the misfortunes that plagued his children. He never accused Koba openly because she had already had her eyes of the night removed by Lawalli several years before. It is possible, too, that since Lawalli had been paid handsomely for curing Koba, he would not have confirmed Kufé's suspicion, had it been brought to him to decide.

In 1966, after Kufé had returned to his original compound, his wife bore him a fourth child who died within a week of its birth. After the death of this infant, Kufé's wife sacrificed to the nightjar and promised to pay if their next child lives. This sacrifice was made to protect against the possibility that she or her husband had unwittingly become contaminated. They consulted no marabout about the death of the fourth child because the mother remembered eating the meat of the dangerous tufted antelope while she was pregnant. Kufé and his wife are now peacefully installed in their original compound with no intention of ever returning to live with Waliba and Abdullae, who still harbors suspicions of adultery.

Through the misfortunes suffered by his children, Kufé was able to withdraw with dignity from an awkward and probably irreconcilable situation. Hard feeling preceded the misfortunes, which was partially ameliorated by Kufé's expeditious departure from a threat of witchcraft. Although it may be argued that this case illustrates tensions beetween affines (Kufé and Koba are in-laws), their relationship to each other seems to have had little or nothing to do with the incident. Only in light of the misunderstanding between Kufé and Abdullae does Kufé's suspicion of Koba make sense. The suspected witch appears not to have been involved in the conflict, but provided a credible target because she lived in the compound that Kufé wished to leave, and because she had been involved several years earlier in a major witchcraft incident. Once Kufé was comfortably reinstalled in his former compound, however, he explained his latest misfortune in terms of mystical contamination, and forgot about witchcraft. Kufé's three consultations with marabouts demonstrate that he merely sought confirmation for what he already believed, and ignored contradictory evidence. As far as Abdullae is concerned, Kufé left because he did not like it there.

CASE 5: CUMPA AND CULONI

Since Culoni created the new compound, he is its headman, and Cumpa, his mother's brother, is his subordinate. The compound includes two very old men who no longer work, the three unmarried sons of one of these elders, Cumpa with his two unmarried sons, Boumbali Nkèta, and Bandia Mamadou, the seer. Except for Boumbali Nkèta (see Case No. 6), all these men work in a single collective field and assist one another in their private peanut fields.

For at least five years, Cumpa has been ailing and steadily losing control of his senses; the last two years he has often been delirious and incapable of working at all. Cumpa has one wife who is perhaps the least attractive woman in the entire village, with whom he argues and exchanges insults daily. He has not slept with her since his sickness became serious, and it is rumored that Cumpa's wife clandestinely favors Culoni, although Culoni has openly supported Cumpa in his domestic disputes. Cumpa remains pagan, although his two sons and Culoni have converted to Islam. Cumpa has lost weight during his illness, his teeth have deteriorated, his hands have lost their strength, his neck and back often ache, and he loses his balance easily. The following account is largely based upon his frequent and liberal testimony.

Culoni has tried to kill Cumpa several times, but so far has failed. Cumpa would like to kill Culoni by sorcery for his witchcraft, but has been unable to do so because Culoni is too well enclosed in his house, which, as Waliba learned, is like an "iron fortress." Indeed, Culoni's house is one of the better built and maintained in the village, with corrugated iron doors that lock, and high, well-kept fences around his back yard. One night Cumpa was crossing the village center to visit his daughter when he heard a noise behind him like a dog running, which passed him going toward the west. This noise, he thought, was a witch. That night he could not sleep, and in the morning a pigeon entered his house by the front door and left by the rear door. He was ill with a swollen stomach and is certain that the pigeon was responsible. The witches said, "Let's kill the soul," but another said, "Leave it for now."

On a later occasion Cumpa passed the village center and someone came to him as a serpent, but it did not dare to come too close because he was carrying a stick. Once he had a cold and vomited a serpent that raised and moved its head, and was certainly something a witch had put in his food.

When he is delirious, he speaks as a Fula Kunda, and he often dreams of red monkeys, cows, a dog, and a cat that want to bite him (all of which, he maintains, are omens of witchcraft). One night an enormous bird passed over his house, which made loud flapping noises with its wings. Cumpa considers himself fortunate that he is not the least bit a seer; otherwise, his soul would have succumbed long ago.

Cumpa learned from a Manding marabout that his problems are definitely due to witchcraft. Two witches are involved, a male and a female. The marabout never specified Culoni, but Cumpa is absolutely certain that it is he. The other witch is of less interest and concern. Once Cumpa's wife fell ill in the rice field, and Cumpa believes that it was because Culoni attacked her as a little whirlwind, perhaps because he had taken credit and needed a soul to repay.

In November 1965, Cumpa consulted a Peul Fouta marabout who was passing the rainy season at Tonghia. The marabout dreamed that Cumpa's soul was attacked one day when he was walking in the bush down the side of a hill by someone who was a whirlwind, who came out of the trees and caused him to fall. He dreamed further that Cumpa's soul was suspended from a tree of the night over water of the night, and that it was tied by the feet, hands, and back of the neck. Heat from the water entered his body and came out of his pores with gases, while his feet dragged in the water. His pain was caused by four cords which encircled his torso. The marabout said that two witches were responsible, a man from Cumpa's own compound and a woman from a neighboring compound.

The Peul Fouta marabout has denied he had made any such diagnosis. He did say, however, that he advised Cumpa to make a sada by pouring water on the threshold of his house and by giving some gunpowder to anyone he wished — by these means, the witches would desist.

On one occasion, Cumpa asked Culoni why he wanted to kill him, and Culoni replied, "Why should I want to kill you? You work for my family." In 1965 Cumpa asked Waliba to reprimand Culoni for his witchcraft, and Waliba did make a public announcement, addressed to no one in particular, that whoever was eating Cumpa should stop. Everyone in the village knows that Cumpa suspects Culoni — Cumpa even claims to know that his tormentor is the chief of all the witches in the village. Others, less involved than Cumpa, suggest that Culoni might be a musician for the chief of the witches. An adolescent boy in Culoni's compound claimed that he had seen Culoni produce clothing from his fingernail!

In terms of kinship propriety, Cumpa is Culoni's elder, but in terms of compound authority, health, industry, and intelligence, Culoni is Cumpa's superior and is envied by him. Apart from the one suggestion of adultery between Culoni and Cumpa's wife (which may have been a joke), there does not seem to have been any serious quarrelling between these two men — and the villagers know of no motive why Culoni would want to eat Cumpa, except perhaps to pay off some credit. Cumpa has had very little to think about during the last several years except his illness and consequent declining fortune. He does gain a great deal of attention through his complaints, and has succeeded in tainting Culoni so that his confidence, industry, and modest wealth all appear to be proof of his evil nature. No concrete evidence has ever been established through a diviner that Culoni is to blame. But Cumpa has the nagging testimony of his own ill health and the precedent of Waliba's former accusations, also unproven, to strengthen his allegations.

CASE 6: A WITHDRAWAL FROM
COLLECTIVE LABORS

In 1965, Boumbali Nkèta and his childless wife withdrew from collective work in Culoni's compound. Although Nkèta continues to live in the compound, his wife cooks and works in his back yard, not in the women's house. Nkèta is younger than Culoni, the headman, and like Waliba, is Culoni's terminological father (*ape*). His wife is a member of the same matrisib as Culoni and Cumpa.

The compound burned some seven years ago, and according to Culoni, Nkèta did not do his share of helping to rebuild it. Culoni chastised Nkèta and thereby angered Nkèta's wife, who exchanged insults with Culoni. She moved out of Culoni's women's house and has not spoken to him since. In 1965, because of constant urging from his wife, Nkèta withdrew from collective labor and made his own corn and millet fields. Soon after his withdrawal, he was immobilized by a severe swelling in his testicles, and passed the whole growing season as an invalid. Despite the existence of tension between the Boumbalis and Culoni, Nkèta's prolonged sickness, a decline in his material fortune, a structural break in social relations, and the immediate presence of a witch (Culoni) who was already believed to be preying upon Cumpa, the issue of witchcraft was never raised. Nkèta did not, to my knowledge, even consult a marabout to explore the possibility.

CASE 7: CRIES IN THE NIGHT

During the period when Cumpa was suffering most from his illness, the nine-year-old son of Culoni was heard crying at night for no apparent reason. The children whispered among themselves that Culoni had tried to eat his son. One adult suggested that Culoni's son is himself a witch, and that his crying was somehow related to that fact.

The son of Culoni is thus suspected of being a witch by some, and the victim of witchcraft by others. Despite the absence of a particular accusation or misfortune, his untimely crying and his close relationship to Culoni have allowed him to be marked by children's speculation. Through nothing more than an innocent coincidence, the boy has become a potential target for future accusations.

CASE 8: CUMPA'S CONSULTATION

In January 1966, after the peanut sales had begun and cash returned to the village, Sekuna, the brother of the marabout Lawalli, appeared at Tonghia. Cumpa, with his eldest son, went to the marabout and declared his suspicions concerning Culoni. Sekuna asked Cumpa if he had ever lost a robe and pair of pants. "Yes," Cumpa said. The marabout then said that Cumpa possesses an instrument that resembles a hand, with five fingers. Cumpa

124

became annoyed and cried, "Me? I never owned such a thing." The marabout asked Cumpa how many spells he knew that could kill someone, do someone harm, or make someone go mad. Cumpa was angry at this and replied, "I don't know any sorcery. I don't see anything. Let me out of here." Sekuna would have struck Cumpa but was prevented from doing so by Waliba. Sekuna continued, "Why did you pierce an egg with a needle at the fork in the path?" Cumpa replied that it was to create trouble between a woman and a man named Mamadi, who competed with Cumpa for the woman. "What happened after you pierced the egg?" asked Sekuna. "He died, but I didn't kill him because he died several years after I did the medicine," said Cumpa. Sekuna declared that it was bow and arrow sorcery (korté). Again he would have struck Cumpa had not Waliba prevented him.

Sekuna said, "Let's go. I don't want to discover any more than that." But Cumpa insisted that he be told who comes to attack him in his house at night. Sekuna asked him what soul credit he had taken. "None," replied Cumpa. Then Sekuna became angry again and ordered Cumpa to remain with him in the house until he declared what credit he had taken that made witches come to his house. Cumpa repeated that he did not have eyes of the night and that he saw nothing. Sekuna asked how he could see witches in his house if he was not a witch himself. Cumpa replied that the witches come as ordinary people, but with no clothing. To get out of this unexpected dilemma, Cumpa paid 1,500 francs ($6) to Sekuna.

This incident was reported to me by mail shortly after I left the field. I do not know if Sekuna was requested, or perhaps even paid, by Culoni to divine what he did. At any rate, he nullified all of Cumpa's previous dreams and consultations with marabouts, and made him responsible for his own suffering. Not only was Cumpa accused of taking credit, but because he had not repaid it, he was a public danger. Cumpa thus learned, for the first time in his life, that he was a witch — and paid the equivalent of six dollars to extricate himself. The sorcery charge was clearly less serious; for Cumpa admitted having done the bow and arrow spell, but would never openly admit witchcraft. This case is unusual in that accuser, victim, and witch are all the same person.

## CASE 9: THE DEATH OF MAIDI

After the departures of Culoni and his followers, and the flight of Kufé who feared for his children, Waliba's compound consisted of himself, his first wife Maidi, his second wife Koba, and his inherited son Abdullae who issued from Maidi's first marriage and who lives with his two wives and an adopted daughter. Three younger men — Tunkan and Karfo who are sister's sons (nimé) of Waliba, and Sanaba who is a distant sibling (fadi) of Waliba — moved into the compound with their young wives.

Abdullae then began to feel more and more estranged within his own family. He complained that Waliba was giving the new arrivals too much attention and that he did not remember or appreciate all the work that Abdullae had done for him in previous years. Abdullae furthermore resented the way in which Waliba neglected Maidi (Abdullae's mother) in favor of Koba, despite the fact that Maidi had been married to him, and thus served him, longer than her co-wife. When Koba complained about family affairs, Waliba was said to have taken her side — with the result that Abdullae eventually told him that he abandons those who have cared for him and embraces those who do not. Abdullae withdrew from his father's collective field and established his own fields and granaries, but continued to live and eat in the compound with the other men. He continued to furnish cooked food for Waliba at every meal and shared with Waliba the support of Maidi. His wives, too, continued to live and eat in the collective house with the other women of the compound. So the kinship pattern of Culoni's departure was partially reversed: previously, the son remained while Waliba's nephews departed; this time, because of the nephews, the son has chosen to withdraw from corporate labors.

In December 1965, Maidi died and her death was preceded by many omens of witchcraft. On the night of November 21, a small owl (cowaeo) called in the village, an indication that a Fula Kunda had come to collect soul credit. On November 22, a young man (Waliba's nimé Tunkan) reported that he had seen a cowaeo on the path to the village of Akan, and speculated in the compound that a woman from Tonghia might have taken credit from witches at Akan because many women from Tonghia had been at Akan in recent days to help the Fula Kunda women harvest rice. From November 23 to 25, Waliba's wife Koba, a renowned witch was at Akan harvesting rice. On the night of November 25, Maidi was in bed with a sore arm, became very sick, and died after a brief but painful illness on the morning of December 3. She was about sixty-five years old.

No mention was made of witchcraft and no accusations were made, despite the presence of a convenient suspect, Koba, who was not on good terms with either Maidi or Abdullae. No connection was ever made between the omens and Maidi's death. When Sekuna, the marabout, came to Tonghia in January, Waliba — not Abdullae — asked about Maidi's death, and was told that she was taken directly by God. Waliba had nothing to gain by pressing the issue of witchcraft, and could have caused his one remaining wife to leave him. The only foreseeable advantage to Abdullae of a witchcraft incident within the compound would be to justify his departure — which he had already accomplished to a very considerable extent.

CASE 10: COWAEO CALLS AGAIN

As it to bear out the Badyaranké belief that witches are most active during the time known as sandiana when the rice is being harvested, another misfortune befell Waliba's compound shortly after Maidi's death. On the night of December 6, Nani, the wife of Tunkan, gave birth to a baby girl. On the night of December 14, the cowaeo was heard to call near the village, and the baby died. Tunkan said explicitly that his wife wished him to consult a marabout, but that he would not do so because he had lost two of three children, and if he were to learn that this was due to witchcraft, it would stir up a great deal of trouble.

Many people probably speculated to themselves that old Koba might have been active again. In this case, I rely to a certain extent on intuition, but suspect that Tunkan chose not to investigate further because he feared witchcraft was involved, and that it would have destroyed his and Waliba's compound. He was disturbed, but the loss was not so great that it merited the undoing of his otherwise harmonious kinship and residential ties.

A rumor began in the compound that Tunkan had resumed sexual relations with Nani too soon after the birth of their last child, who was about two years old — and that the baby and the child who also became ill were suffering from mystical contamination. Thus, in a context where knowledge of witchcraft seems to have been unwanted, but where the evidence for witchcraft was clearly apparent, the inadvertent violation of a taboo emerged as one possible explanation.

CASE 11: TO THE BRINK AND BACK

A three-year-old boy, the child of Sanaba and Alarba of Waliba's compound, became ill and swollen during January 1966 shortly after the above-mentioned series of misfortunes. This event caused some uneasiness because Sanaba consulted a marabout who said that the illness was caused by a dark old woman of Sanaba's own compound. He made no incident, however, and visited a second marabout who told him that his child suffered a sickness that was not due to any malevolent agencies. When Sekuna arrived in January, he was asked to divine the source of the child's illness. Waliba, Sanaba, Karfo, and Emile (my assistant who described the event in a letter) went together to pose the question. Sekuna looked at his Koran and said, "Many people say it is witches, others say it is the mother, others say it is the father, but me, in my Koran, I don't see that the child has been the victim of a witch. The child is the victim of a hot breeze." (This is the breeze that is believed to carry contagious danger, which originates in quarrelling, to children.) He recommended that Sanaba pass around five red kola nuts as a sada. But because red kola nuts are associated with death, Sanaba passed around five white kola nuts instead.

In this case, sickness itself nearly caused what would have been a serious blow to compound unity, especially after the first marabout's diagnosis. As in the preceding case involving Tunkan,

128

Sanaba seems to have tried to avoid accusing Koba and through two more inquiries with diviners arrived at an acceptable answer. There was a little tension in the compound and there had been some of the usual quarrelling in the women's house, which could plausibly have contaminated the air and thereby the child. Sanaba was prompted to investigate the cause of the sickness because he wanted a healthy child — not to instigate a witch-hunt. Sanaba and Tunkan seemed to choose not to increase the sadness felt by Waliba over the loss of Maidi, by not subjecting his one remaining wife to intimidation and possible expulsion from the compound. The misfortunes and omens which occurred were not sufficient to destroy what solidarity remained within Waliba's family.

CASE 12: WALI AND THE POISONED SOUL

When the elder Wali died, three persons, including his sister's daughter Koba (Case 4) and Satio (Case 13) were accused by Lawalli the marabout of causing the death by witchcraft. Within one week after Wali's death, Koba's married daughter who resided in Wali's compound dropped dead while walking through the village center at night. It is believed by many in the village that her death was somehow linked with his.

Koba's son said that Wali possessed many medicines and some were intended to poison anyone who ate his soul. Also he said because it is natural for a mother to feed her daughter, Koba probably gave part of Wali's soul to her daughter who ate it and died, and since the three witches are still living, they may not have actually eaten the soul themselves.

The death of Koba's daughter was never brought to a marabout, or if it was, the knowledge so gained was never made public. Her death was viewed by some as a form of justice, as well as the proof of her guilt.

CASE 13: SATIO THE BIRD

Satio, like Koba, acquired his major reputation for witchcraft when Lawalli accused them and one other person of having killed Wali. Satio, now headman of what remains of Wali's compound, is one of the three important blacksmiths of the village, a non-Moslem, and a celebrated hunter. During my fieldwork, he killed a lion and a panther, each at night and each with a single ball from his homemade muzzle-loader. He spends many hours by himself in the forest collecting sap for palm wine by day and hunting wild animals at night; he is said to be a successful hunter because he can turn himself into a certain species of bird and alight on the limb of a tree until game comes near, whereupon he transforms himself back into a man to fire the fatal shot. In other respects, Satio is a poor cultivator, has a nervous disposition, and is frequently drunk.

When Satio was a young man, even before the death of Wali, he is said to have attacked one of his work partners during the period of sandiana while doing wage labor at Thiés. This partner was a distant sibling of Satio and also a blacksmith. At Tonghia they had neither lived nor worked together, nor had they experienced any particularly close or strained rapport. Satio's alleged victim revealed that Satio had attacked him three times in the form of a large bird, which the victim, being a seer, successfully fought off. The third time the bird attacked, the victim seized and beat it until it vomited and urinated blood. Satio and this man are not on speaking terms as a consequence of this mysterious event.

Subsequent to the death of Wali, Satio's first wife died in childbirth. Satio sent Brahima, his full brother, to learn from Lawalli why his wife had died. Lawalli informed Brahima that Satio had eaten his own wife's soul. Lawalli added that Satio had taken soul credit with a certain Fula Kunda for whom he forged iron tools. Lawalli invited Satio to surrender his "knife of the night," but Satio refused.

No one at Tonghia knows of any motives based upon prior conflicts in social relations between Satio and his working partner, and Satio and his late wife. Because of his long association with affairs of the night, his courageous successes in the hunt reflect upon him as evidence of his evil commitments. Rather than admiration, he reaps gossip and suspicion. It is significant that Satio is said to have taken credit with a Fula Kunda witch.

Blacksmiths are the only Badyaranké with enduring social and economic ties with the Fula Kunda, and in the cases of Satio and Kokudo (Case 15), the tie is believed to extend to the invisible world.

Although Brahima, who lives in Satio's compound, has never been directly implicated in witchcraft accusations, he is said by many villagers to be a potential eater of souls. One informant complained that when there is a plate of meat to be eaten, Brahima swallows more than his share and then, like a cow, withdraws to chew. Despite the absence of any specific charges against him, Brahima is said by many to be one of the major witches of the village.

Brahima's wife, Mokuto, lost two infant children, and one village informant said that some believe that Satio ate his brother's children's souls. Mokuto believes that she was contaminated by the fédé (nightjar). She said that when the first child died, she intentionally killed the fédé to be certain she was contaminated; then she made a libation to the bird's shrine and promised to pay if the next child lived. A second child was born and subsequently died. Mokuto claims that the second child died because she forgot to pay the shrine. A third child was born, she sacrificed two fowl to the shrine, and the child is still living. The third living child, she reasoned, is proof that the previous two had died because of contamination. No marabout was consulted about the deaths of the two children, and had Lawalli been consulted, her brother-in-law Satio would conceivably have been blamed. Witchcraft never reared its head, despite the suggestive presence of Satio and Brahima.

Kosita, an adult male resident of Satio's compound, confided that Satio had twice attempted to kill him by witchcraft. Once, as he was walking on a forest path, Satio tried to bite him as a serpent, but he escaped. On the second occasion, Satio invited him to go to the fields and arranged an ambush by witches; Satio turned himself into a black bird and flew over Kosita's head, thus frightening him into returning to the village. Kosita explained that he knows the snake and black bird were Satio because it was revealed to him in a dream, not because he is a seer. Kosita moved out of Satio's compound in 1966; he said that he wished to move because he feared witchcraft from Satio and Brahima. On a later occasion, he said that witchcraft had nothing to do with his intention to move, and that he had no way of knowing if Satio or Brahima were witches. He has never attributed any particular misfortune of his own to them. Kosita also has said that he wished to establish a new compound because he was more prosperous than Satio and Brahima, and feared their envy. Kosita belongs to the matrisib of Satio's father and Satio is his son. Although Kosita's departure severed his attenuated patrilineal or affinal ties to Satio and Brahima, he took two men with him who were related patrilineally and as affines.

CASE 14: UNAR'S STICK OF THE NIGHT

The compound of Caparing had once been populous at Tonghia, but over the years people moved away or died, leaving only one old man named Konya, his wife, and Tunkan, his sister's son. Next door, in another small compound lived Camusu with his wife and two young sons (one of whom was named Unar). Konya, Camusu, and Unar were not closely related. Konya's wife died, leaving only him and Tunkan in the compound. Konya became ill with an unpleasant stomach disorder and announced that young Unar was trying to kill him; he claimed he had been sleeping under the eaves of his house when Unar came to injure him with a "stick of the night."

Tunkan, at the time of Konya's sickness, had been doing wage labor in the north of Senegal. Learning of Konya's accusation when he returned, Tunkan beat Unar, and told Camusu in no uncertain terms that if Konya died, he would hold his son responsible for the death. Unar fled to his grandmother's compound in Guinea. Later on, Unar returned to Tonghia, and eventually Konya died from his stomach trouble. At the time of his death, he was preparing to move into Camusu's compound because Tunkan had moved into Waliba's. No one seems to know if Konya died of witchcraft or of natural causes; he made no accusations, and no one attempted to determine if witchcraft was involved.

Konya was said to have been on good terms with Camusu and

Unar before his death. As was apparently the case in Moussa's death (Case 19), the death of an isolated old man with no survivors or dependents required no explanation. Unar had been accused while the ailing Konya was alive, and Tunkan was obliged to act in his behalf; in death, however, the question of blame was ignored. Unar's early association with affairs of the night is, nevertheless, inerasable, and he is still thought by many to be a powerful witch. (In 1970 I received a letter from Tonghia notifying me that he had been beaten and driven from the village because of an accusation of witchcraft.)

CASE 15: KOKUDO LOSES A WIFE

Kokudo was born in Kankelifa in Portuguese Guinea. While he was still a young man he moved to the compound of Sandé Kunda at Tonghia, where his mother's brother was headman. When Kokudo's younger brother Sutra came from Kankelifa to join him, Kokudo withdrew from the collective field of the compound to make a field with his brother; both, however, resided in the compound. The compound of Sandé Kunda contained a number of blacksmiths, and both Kokudo and Sutra were smiths.

Kokudo asked for the hand of the daughter of an old man living in his compound, and eventually she became Kokudo's second wife. According to widespread village rumor, Kokudo was unable to satisfy the sexual needs of his new wife, and she abandoned him. Kosita (see Case 13), a man from a compound on the other side of the village, made Kokudo's runaway wife pregnant and married her. Kokudo did not ask for his bridewealth to be returned, although it was his right to do so. He and Sutra left the compound and began their own on the other side of the village.

Several months after Kokudo moved into his new compound, his former father-in-law died. The father-in-law had been visiting a nearby Fula Kunda village where he became ill, presumably from something he had eaten. His son, Kokudo's former brother-in-law, consulted the marabout Lawalli concerning the cause of the death. The information he obtained was ambiguous, but he nevertheless suspected that Kokudo had caused his father's death by witchcraft. One self-designated authority on the incident explained that Kokudo feared killing the elder unaided, so he elicited the assistance of a Fula Kunda witch who was his friend and for whom he made tools. The old man's son never announced his suspicion because he did not wish to create trouble; the suspicion is known, however, to everyone in the village. Kosita, who took Kokudo's wife, revealed that a marabout had informed him that Kokudo has tried to use sorcery to kill him.

In summary, Kokudo's wife left him for reasons that he did not care to plead before the elders, and his bridewealth was never returned. In this case, a clear motive was attributable to the suspected witch—he killed his father-in-law because of an unresolved breach of marital contract. Kokudo's affines, by accusing him of witchcraft, dispensed with any unfulfilled obligation which they may have felt toward him. As was the case with Satio, Kokudo, a blacksmith, was believed to have enlisted the cooperation of his Fula Kunda client. (Cooperation between witches follows the patterns of normal social relations.)

While living in his new compound, Kokudo lost a daughter who had been engaged to a Badyaranké from the village of Sare Oura. The bereaved young man learned from Lawalli that Kokudo had eaten the soul of his daughter. Kokudo and his wife left Tonghia to see Lawalli and remained away for two years. They were said not to have had 5,000 francs ($20) to pay Lawalli to remove Kokudo's eyes of the night, so they were obliged to work in Tambacounda to accumulate the necessary amount. In 1965 Kokudo returned to Tonghia, presumably without his eyes of the night. No motive has been entertained by anyone as to why Kokudo ate his daughter's soul.

Kokudo's brother Sutra and his eldest son Cumba are believed by many to be witches. When Cumba's youngest brother was undergoing his circumcision ordeal, Kamara Paiti, the seer, announced that Cumba tried to kill his young brother while in the form of a kettle. The next year Cumba's wife died unexpectedly for unknown reasons. After Paiti's accusation and his wife's mysterious death, Cumba has been wandering nomadically from village to village.

Kokudo's second eldest son, Bokari, lives today in the compound with Kokudo and Sutra. In 1965 Bokari's three-year-old son died, and Bokari admitted that he had broken the postpartum sex taboo, and thus supposedly poisoned the child by poisoning its mother's milk. It is not known if Bokari believed this explanation of his son's death, and it is not certain that the child was actually feeding from its mother at the time. If Bokari had been curious about witches and consulted a marabout, however, he might have learned that Kokudo or Sutra, his two closest fathers, were responsible. Through these episodes, it is evident Kokudo's reputation for witchcraft spread almost as a contagious disease over his most immediate kinsmen.

CASE 16: TONTO'S CHILDREN

Tonto is one of the most respectable people at Tonghia and heads the largest unified compound in the village. Abelle, one of his four wives, has lost seven infant children. After the death of the seventh, Abelle asked her husband to ask the marabout Lawalli for an explanation. Tonto sent two young men to Lawalli who informed them, "He who sent you has eaten his son." Abelle threatened to leave Tonto when she heard of this, and he had to use much persuasion to keep her. Eventually Abelle had a living child, and the accusation was forgotten.

Tonto is still whispered to be a witch by children; all the adults know the story, but he is not considered evil and people do not fear him. Witchcraft beliefs combined with a series of misfortunes threatened to dissolve an otherwise stable marriage — but because of its stability, the witchcraft was more or less ignored. Tonto himself said that his wife was bothered by genies who kill her children. On one occasion, the genies were driven out by an injection she received at a hospital in Guinea.

CASE 17: THE DEATH OF TOTALA

A young man named Totala left Tonghia with his wife and another young man to grow peanuts for one year in the country of the Diola. In June 1965, his wife and the young man returned to Tonghia to report Totala's untimely death. According to their account, Totala gave his wife the bark of a certain tree to prepare as a medicine for him to drink. After he took the medicine, he became paralyzed and died shortly afterwards. He had taken this same medicine many times before, so either it was improperly prepared or someone had poisoned it. Totala's older brother (Pedebo) went secretly to consult the marabout Sekuna, and learned the names of three witches, all residents of Tonghia, who had killed his brother. The older brother has refused to admit he consulted a marabout, and has not divulged the names of the witches.

Totala had been paying bridewealth for a young lady in Culoni's compound to her mother's brother, Mamadou. Pedebo chose to inherit the engagement to this girl and continued to perform services and make payments. Pedebo has said privately that the marabout told him that his brother was shot by a "gun of the night," and that one of the witches lives in the compound with his prospective wife. He has chosen to keep this knowledge to himself because he fears he would spoil his still tenuous claim to the girl if he openly accuses the witch in her compound. For this reason he has been unwilling to talk about the cause of his brother's death. After all, he said, Totala's first wife (who prepared the medicine) had lost one other husband before she married Totala — she might have a genie who kills her husbands.

Thus Pedebo seems to have rejected powerful evidence of witchcraft because it is to his advantage to do so. At the same time, he has more or less convinced himself that it was due to a mysterious genie, for which no one can be blamed. This interpretation allows Pedebo a side benefit: he did not wish to inherit Totala's first wife, and her supposed anti-husband genie gave him a good reason to refuse.

CASE 18: THE BIOGRAPHY OF
WOKO THE WITCH

Woko is the most famous witch in the history of Tonghia, and his was always the first name to be volunteered by informants when questioned about witchcraft. His reputation began when he was still a young boy returning with two other boys from arduous labors in the peanut fields near Thiés. Woko, Fatiba who was older, and Ngaling who was younger had all worked together as a team and were hiking to Tonghia with their luggage on their heads. Fatiba, a known seer, perceived that the two younger men had tried once and failed to take his soul; they tried a second time during the trek and this time he believed they succeeded. Fatiba was bearing the heaviest part of the luggage, since he was older and stronger; he believed they had concealed his soul in the trunk carried on his head. When they arrived at Tonghia, Fatiba was very sick and said, "If I am dead, these two are responsible."

Ngaling fled, but Woko was tied in the chief's compound and questioned by the elder men; he denied his guilt and was beaten. He was then brought to the ailing Fatiba and ordered by the elders to cure him. Badyaranké believe a soul can be restored by touching the head and body of the victim and by blowing in his ear and on his body. But Woko refused. Then he confessed that he had been sent by his father to kill Fatiba and did not dare cure him. His father said, "Yes; it is true. I have the soul, but it is already dead." Woko and his father were beaten, and two days later Fatiba died. Woko was subsequently attacked by two people with sticks and reportedly attempted suicide. He finally left Tonghia and lived for three years in Gambia.

When Woko returned to Tonghia, he settled peacefully with his father in a new compound. A young girl of the same matrisib as the dead Fatiba fell sick, accused Woko of killing her, and died. Neither the girl nor Fatiba were relatives of Woko, but they came from the same part of the village. When the girl's brother Moussa returned from military service, he tried to shoot Woko; he fled again to Gambia for four years.

While in Gambia, Woko is said to have killed another young man named Sare. Sare had gone to harvest palm wine, and Woko followed him. Sare's younger brother said, "Chase Woko away. He is up to something." Both brothers were seers. Sare said, "No. Let Woko do as he wants." Sare died and Woko is believed to have been responsible.

Woko again returned to Tonghia. A young woman, Moussa's wife, sickened, and claimed she was shot by a "gun of the night."

Woko was no relative of the woman, but Moussa suspected that Woko had given soul credit to the girl's mother, who then killed her own daughter to repay. The mother reportedly said to her daughter, "If you die, die like a sheep without saying anything." Although Moussa believes that Woko in collusion with the mother caused the woman's death, no marabout was consulted and nothing was done.

Woko was suspected of involvement in other deaths as well, but his most serious incident was also his last at Tonghia. A young unmarried man named Sunkaru was returning from the fields one evening and was attacked by the sister's son (nimé) of Woko named Alimu. Alimu, himself a young man, had waited in ambush near the path and had thrown himself at Sunkaru when he passed. Sunkaru, a powerful seer, knocked Alimu down. A third young man, Padiare, of the same matrisib as Alimu, had been defecating in the bush and came to Alimu's assistance. He hit Sunkaru on the back of the head with a "stick of the night." Alimu took Sunkaru's soul and they fled. Alimu asked his mother to guard the soul for him in her earthen storage urn; she said it would be unsafe and he should give it to Woko, her brother. Woko took the soul and suspended it from a mango tree. Alimu left for Velingara, after having arranged a date with Woko when they would kill the soul.

Sunkaru returned to the village after the attack feeling ill, did not eat that night, and the following morning accused Alimu and Woko of having stolen his soul. He said, "Call Alimu," but Alimu was not there. He said, "Call Padiare," and the men of the village called him, but he denied the accusation. Padiare was tied up and left in the sun. Padiare said, "Call Woko." Woko tried to get away but was brought to the compound of Sunkaru's father where he had been beaten during the sickness of Fatiba many years before. Woko denied that he had anything to do with the theft of Sunkaru's soul. Padiare said that Woko was not there at the time, but that he now had the soul. Woko continued to deny the accusation, until Alimu himself had been found and tied up. Padiare said, "I helped Alimu because Sunkaru would have killed him. I didn't want the soul." Alimu then said that he had given the soul to Woko.

The men of the village took Woko to search for the soul. Woko said that he had found it and cupped his hands, but Sunkaru, the seer, knew that he was faking. So they placed a split bamboo over Woko's head like a big clothespin and led him and Padiare to the mango tree. Woko said he could not climb the tree with the bamboo on his head, so they lifted him and put him in the tree. Several seers from the village came along as guides, and through them the men learned of the whereabouts of the soul in the tree. While Woko was in the tree, they asked Padiare if Woko had found the soul, and Padiare said, "Yes." The people asked Woko to show them, but he refused to open his hand. Woko then touched between the shoulders of the sick Sunkaru and he was cured. The elders told Woko that if Sunkaru was ever sick again he would be responsible. Woko left to complain to the Prefect at Velingara; he was judged to be right in the Prefect's eyes because "the Government doesn't believe you can kill someone without a gun or a knife." Sunkaru, his father, and three other men who beat Woko were put in prison at Velingara for the duration of the dry season.

Woko and his wife, Alimu and his wife, and Alimu's mother left Tonghia and moved permanently to the village of Sare Oura in 1958. They remained as guests in a compound at Sare Oura for one year, and the issue of witchcraft was raised again. So Woko built his own compound with Alimu and several younger men. He lives there today, at the age of about fifty-five, a respectable compound headman.

This case has been constructed and confirmed by interviews with at least six people. Several, including Sunkaru's father and brother were asked why Woko and Alimu attacked Sunkaru. The answer was always that they did not know. Sunkaru was no relative of the witches, came from the opposite side of the village, was neither their friend nor their enemy, had never been in competition with them over women, and had never fought with them. All said that the attack was unexpected and that it would not have been suspected had not Sunkaru himself cited his attackers. They were not altogether surprised, however, for they knew Woko had many similar episodes in his past and said that "he has no shame." Absolutely no one talks about these matters with Woko (including the ethnographer), who is for the first time living in tranquility. He visits Tonghia often; relatives from Tonghia go to visit him and eat food in his house.

Woko's first accusation may have been explicable in terms of some unknown or forgotten quarrel between him and the elder Fatiba — but if so, it happened many years ago and no one remembers. His subsequent involvement in one incident after another, culminating in Sunkaru's sickness, does not appear to have been related to competitive or conflict-laden social relationships. Woko became a target for a whole series of unexplained and unpleasant misfortunes that demanded explanations. He became so well known that even the behavior of other witches was blamed on him, as in the case of the woman believed to have eaten her daughter because she owed him credit. Woko found himself with many passionate enemies in the village whose anger derived from their belief that he was a witch, not from previous tensions, misunderstandings, or disputes. Woko was certainly a scapegoat, although not exactly in the sense that Kluckhohn had in mind when he wrote: "Navahos blame their trouble on witches instead of upon 'Jews' or 'niggers'." [4] Woko was not an outsider, for witches among the Badyaranké are close neighbors, friends, or relatives — or more accurately, belief in witchcraft provides a means of converting a friend, neighbor, or relative into an outsider. As his reputation snowballed, his father and, toward the end of his career, his sister and two of his sister's sons became associated with the evils of witchcraft.

CASE 19: THE DEATHS OF
SUNKARU AND MOUSSA

Sunkaru, the victim of Woko's last witchcraft incident at Tonghia, crossed the frontier to work in Guinea, where he became very sick and died, though still a young man. Despite the warning given

[4] 1944:90.

140

Woko by the village elders, Woko was not blamed for the death. According to village lore, Sunkaru had been courting the wife of a marabout who, after repeated warnings, did something to Sunkaru's name that caused him to sicken and die. Because witchcraft and sorcery are complementary and exclusive explanations for misfortune, Woko was absolved from responsibility for Sunkaru's death.

Moussa, whose mother's brother, sister, and wife had presumably died from Woko's hands, was living as a celibate widower in 1965. Although he was approximately forty-five years old, he was living in relative poverty, without dignity, in a collective house for young boys. In September 1965, Moussa was stricken with severe liver pains and died after a short but agonizing illness. Although dogs howled during the week of his illness (an omen of witchcraft) and although Woko himself was visiting the village during that same week, he was never suspected or accused of meddling in Moussa's unexpected death.

A joking partner (sunaho) of Moussa who came to Tonghia to attend the funeral offered an explanation that some villagers seem to have accepted without question. The visitor recollected how, many years before, Moussa had made a request at a shrine (koasé) in Guinea, and promised to pay with a goat if he enjoyed a safe journey back to Tonghia. Although he arrived safely, no one knows whether or not he actually fulfilled his promise to the shrine. One of the mourners argued that a shrine notifies its debtor by burning his house three times and kills only as a last resort. Since Moussa's house did not burn, someone speculated that poison might have been put in Moussa's food on a former and forgotten occasion: "Some poisons take years to act while they grow inside the victim as a lizard or serpent, which eats the vital organs." One villager said he believed that Moussa died because of something "stronger" than poison. But the matter was left open, and no one inquired any further.

Several factors may have influenced the blamelessness of Moussa's death. Woko was no longer living at Tonghia and had severed his social relationships there. Moussa himself had declined in social importance, almost to the point of being considered as a troublesome child. Furthermore, he was one of the last of his matrisib in the village and had no close relatives who might have taken the initiative to inquire on his behalf. Finally, when he died, the brother (fadi) of Woko was the only witness to his last words, and he might not have mentioned an accusation had it been made. This case also reveals that it is easier to avoid a witchcraft incident if the victim simply dies; whereas, had Moussa made accusations while ill, they would have been difficult to ignore. His death was not socially disruptive, he had few survivors, and no attempt was made to allocate blame.

CASE 20: OLD WASSA'S SORCERY

Niaboli Wassa, the oldest living person in Tonghia, reminisced one day about how he had once eliminated some of his in-laws by sorcery. For unexplained reasons, his mother-in-law broke up his marriage with her daughter, and he went to a marabout to seek revenge. The marabout saw that Wassa was angry and said, "What shall I do for you?" Wassa replied he wanted his wife's mother killed. The marabout asked Wassa for a chicken, over which he uttered a verse that caused the chicken to die; he then told Wassa if he completed that particular sorcery, not only the mother, but also the new husband and all of his successors would die. Wassa said that he did not care; they could all die as far as he was concerned. The mother became blind and all the inheritors of the women eventually died — a not inexplicable outcome, since Wassa has outlived everyone in the area.

This reminiscence points out that sorcery, unlike witchcraft, is a relative evil and is occasionally admitted. An additional interpretation, only partially verified, is that Wassa admitted his sorcery to avoid being suspected of having done the same deeds by witchcraft.

CASE 21: ALINTU THE MONKEY

Alintu is an attractive young woman about twenty-five years old; she came to Tonghia from Guinea to be the second wife of Kamara Arfan. In Guinea, people believed she changed into a monkey and even into a tree full of monkeys, especially during the critical period of sandiana. How she originally acquired this reputation is forgotten or unknown. Her unfortunate loss of two infant children at Tonghia confirms widespread suspicion that she is an eater of souls.

Any explanation for Alintu's suspected dark deeds lies outside of her present family situation and has nothing to do with pre-existing tensions between her and her husband, children, co-wives, or neighbors. In this case, the belief that Alintu is a witch may generate tensions, rather than serve as an idiom for formulating tensions already present. In 1965 she delivered a third child. Of the fate of this child, one suspicious villager said, "Let us wait and see."

INTERPRETATION OF CASE MATERIAL

Although Evans-Pritchard's pioneering distinction between witch-craft and sorcery was intended to represent Zande concepts in English translation, ne'er-do-wells- from other cultures around the earth have been inconsiderately lumped together under these two labels for purposes of consistency and cross-cultural comparison. The authors of the introductory essays in *African Systems of Thought* went so far as to specify a list of criteria to which aspiring witches and sorcerers must conform, in order to deserve membership in one or the other of these categories.[5] John Middleton and E. H. Winter in their Introduction to

---

[5] M. Fortes and G. Dieterlen (1965:23–24) make these distinctions:

"1. The sorcerer uses magic to perpetrate his evil deeds; whereas the witch is effective by having a special type of personality.

"2. People who are sorcerers are conscious of their actions and deliberate in their intentions; whereas those who are witches may not know of the evil life they lead after normal waking hours, and, even if they do, may be driven by an uncontrollable urge.

"3. The sorcerer may be driven by anger, envy, or malice of a passing kind; whereas the witch has a permanent addiction to his anti-social actions, one that is rooted in heredity or in early conditioning.

"4. The actions of the sorcerer, depending as they do on material substances and/or specific verbal magic, are not as baffling to ordinary minds as are the supernatural machinations of the witch.

"5. The ethnographer can usually believe that sorcery is attempted (even though he may not accept allegations regarding its prevalence or its effectiveness); whereas he can only dismiss as fantastic the idea that witchcraft is even practised, let alone that it is effective."

*Witchcraft and Sorcery in East Africa* suggested that these contrasting phenomena might engage themselves in different ways with the social structure, and thus fulfill separate sociological functions. A number of Africanists [6] have described ethnographic contexts where the anthropologists' distinction between witch and sorcerer was not made clear by the native speakers, or the two were amalgamated to varying degrees. Because the terms do not refer to any self-evident class of phenomena outside of Zande culture, and because no convincing sociological correlations have been demonstrated that would justify a formalized usage, *sorcerer* and *witch* might better be considered, as Mary Douglas [7] has suggested, as content-free labels for ethnographic entities which should be specified in each case. Following a suggestion from Douglas's "Witch Beliefs in Central Africa," I have been attentive to the varying extents to which the two principal types of mystical evil-doers known to the Badyaranké (referred to herein as witch and sorcerer) provide blame-pinning explanations for misfortune. In addition to the different cultural attributes associated with Badyaranké witches and sorcerers, they are also being considered from the point of view of their feedback on social relations. To be accused of sorcery is far less serious and disruptive than to be accused of witchcraft.

Anthropological theories about blame-pinning explanations of misfortune that involve mystical agents (i.e., the literature on witchcraft and sorcery) have addressed both cultural and sociological questions. In the former category, Kluckhohn, Middleton, [8] and others have pointed out how witchcraft beliefs essentially "assert by condemning their opposite the values of the society where the assertion is being made." [9] The observation that witchcraft and related beliefs reinforce social norms has also been made by Bronislaw Malinowski, Guy Swanson, and Beatrice Whiting.[10]

Evans-Pritchard demonstrated that such beliefs provide an

[6] Beidelman 1963:57–98; Hulstaert 1965:165–170; Huntingford 1963:175–186; Krige and Krige 1943:250; Marwick 1965a:73–83.
[7] 1967:73.
[8] Kluckhohn 1962:110–113; Middleton 1963:271.
[9] Mair 1969:203.
[10] Malinowski 1926:93–94; Swanson 1964:137–152; Whiting 1950:69.

intellectual comfort to the individual Azande, who requires a personal explanation for misfortune, illness, and death. The indifferent succession of health and decay is made, if not less inevitable, at least understandable, and subject to punitive sanctions within the social group itself. This intellectualistic interpretation, conceived by Lucien Levy-Bruhl, independently expressed by Clyde Kluckhohn, and argued by J. Clyde Mitchell in his "A Note on the African Conception of Causality" [11] has proven to be one of the soundest observations of the function of witchcraft. "My own view would be," wrote Lucy Mair, "that the functional explanation is valid only in connection with the ascription of misfortune to witchcraft; people do 'have to' have an explanation of their misfortunes." [12] The fact that people have to have an explanation of their misfortunes, however, does not help us to sort out which unfortunate events are explained by witchcraft, and under what circumstances.

Sociological theories have generally sought to demonstrate that witchcraft and sorcery accusations provide a convenient vantage point for locating areas of tension and interpersonal conflict, and that such accusations make an ultimately beneficial contribution to social well-being. Numerous writers have maintained that mystical, blame-pinning accusations reflect tense social relationships. [13] Several writers have also maintained that such accusations serve to resolve such tense relationships. [14] M. G. Marwick, for example, writes that "accusations of witchcraft and sorcery are indices of tense social relationships between the accuser, on the one hand, and the sorcerer or witch on the other," [15] that such accusations "blast down the dilapidated parts of the social structure and clear the rubble in preparation for the development of new . . . ones," [16] and that such beliefs pro-

[11] 1952:51–58.
[12] 1969:211.
[13] Basso 1969:55; Douglas 1967:72–80; Evans-Pritchard 1937:105–106; Krige 1947:17; Kuper 1965:175; Maybury-Lewis 1967:274–278; Nadel 1952: 28; Schapera 1952:49.
[14] Gluckman 1963:81–108; Marwick 1952, 1965a, 1965b; Mitchell 1956: 131–182; Turner 1957:131–168.
[15] 1965b:171.
[16] 1952:232.

vide "a means by which redundant, insupportable relationships, which through being close and personal cannot be quietly contracted out of, are dramatically blasted away." [17]

Ames, Douglas, [18] and Turner have criticized this overly optimistic conception of the positive value of witchcraft and sorcery. David Ames writes of the Wolof, close neighbors of the Badyaranké, that

. . . beliefs about [witches] operate at best as an imperfect explanation and means of control over human ailments. Since today these appear to make for social conflicts and to produce anxieties more often than to reduce them, the Wolof [witchcraft] complex can be regarded as mainly dysfunctional, both in the social and psychological sense.[19]

Victor Turner observed in an article on the general subject of witchcraft and sorcery that

If witch beliefs were solely the product of social tensions and conflicts they would betray their origins by possessing a more markedly rational form and content. Constant exposure to ugly illness and sudden death, and the need to adapt to them swiftly, have surely contributed to the formation of these ugly and irrational beliefs. And once formed the beliefs feed back into the social process, generating tensions as often as "reflecting" them.[20]

The Badyaranké material supports these three authors' reservations toward a too uncritical association of witchcraft and sorcery with necessary or constructive realignments in the social order. Furthermore, although it is certainly true that conflict and hard feelings will be found where accusations are being made, the considerations in each case should be whether the hard feelings anticipated the accusation, or were, in fact, generated by the accusation.

Each of the explanations that the Badyaranké recognize, and from which they choose, embodies different implications for the behavior of those who are most directly concerned with the misfortune. These explanations range between witchcraft, at

17 1965a:147.
18 1963.
19 Ames 1959:273.
20 Turner 1964:315–316.

one extreme, which provides a powerful incentive to pin blame on someone in the community, and at the other extreme, inadvertent violations of pollution taboos, genies in the head, forgotten contracts with shrines, and direct acts of God, which contain and eliminate blame. Sorcery (the punishment for which tends to be in kind), contracts with sprites, and individual affairs with genies (which invite mild censure but no punishment) lie in that order between these two extremes.

The contexts in which witchcraft (an inherent power, combined with a distinctive soul, capacity for vision into an otherwise invisible world, and an ability to transform oneself) and sorcery (a mechanical process, generally dispensed for a fee by a marabout to his clients) occur among the Badyaranké reveal a few slight gradations of difference. I was able to determine with reasonable assurance whether or not some objective evidence of hard feeling had preceded accusations of witchcraft in twenty-six incidents, and of these, only six clearly displayed prior conflict. These conflicts include Waliba's envy and resentment of the growing autonomy of one of the younger men in his compound (Case 2), fear of betrayal by Abdullae who believed that his friend Kufé had committed adultery with one of his two wives (Case 4), an unfulfilled obligation by Kokudo's in-laws who did not return his bridewealth after the embarrassing loss of his wife to another man (Case 15), and the seer Paiti's fear of reprisal by the angry husband whose wife he had stolen. In an extensive case referred to in this chapter (Case 12), an elder named Wali, headman of a large compound, died at a ripe old age. His son learned from a marabout that the death was caused by three witches, two of whom were in the compound, and one of whom had argued with the elder on occasion about collective labors. Two of the witches (including Koba but not Satio, the one with whom the elder quarrelled) were punished, and the compound divided into several new compounds. In the sixth incident, not in the case section of the chapter, an elder had sympathized with his daughter in her rejection of a spouse and of a would-be spouse. When this elder died, it was believed by his son that the two frustrated men had killed him through an elaborate attack of witchcraft. Nothing, however, was done to these two men except to tarnish their reputations. Five of the six incidents followed misfortunes (that involving Paiti excepted), and in these five incidents, witchcraft beliefs did facilitate the breaking off of relationships that at one time had been intimate, but had become unpleasantly strained. In these cases, Marwick's image of "insupportable relationships" being "blasted away" and the Badyaranké belief that witches choose some victims because of anger would seem appropriate.

In the majority of witchcraft cases, it is difficult to demonstrate that interpersonal antagonisms generated suspicion and erupted into accusation, or that such suspicion and accusation could have effected subsequent relationships in some constructive way. In Cumpa's case, for example, his persistent illness suggested the possibility of witchcraft; and Culoni, a known witch in the same compound, became more and more hated as the illness intensified. Cumpa, nevertheless, wanted to regain his health, not to become headman or move to another compound. Likewise, the alienation of Tamba and Diandian from Culoni (Case 3) was a consequence of a series of harsh misfortunes and not an expression of familial discontent. Suspicion of Culoni's child grew out of nothing more than children's speculation. Responsibility for the death of Totala (Case 17), said to be the result of witchcraft by the most reliable marabout and gravely disturbing to his brother who had inquired in reaction to grief and not out of malice, was suppressed in order not to create tensions with the alleged witch. The death of Tonto's children (Case 16) nearly wrecked a marriage that was otherwise satisfactory; and the sickness of Sanaba's and Tunkan's children (Cases 11 and 10) caused some tense moments in Waliba's peaceful compound.

As would be expected from Badyaranké theory about witchcraft motives — and in most of the investigated incidents — witches did not always bewitch those whom they hated (motives based upon tense social relations were infrequently attributed to the witch). The sorrowful histories of Culoni, Woko, Kokudo, Satio, and Koba suggest that persons, after being accused once for whatever reason, may become the scapegoats for any suffering which occurs near them. Accusations against these famous witches snowballed because of an increasingly self-perpetuating conviction that they were witches, not because of quarrels or antisocial behavior on their part. The stigma attached to Culoni, Woko, Kokudo, Satio, and Koba even contaminated some of their closest kin.

Suspicions and accusations also may be drummed up arbitrarily by marabouts and seers. Paiti, for example, caused hard feelings between two brothers with whom he had no quarrel and to whom he was not related because he claimed to "see" the older brother attempt to kill the younger while transformed as a kettle. This accusation was plausible to the villagers because Kokudo, the father of the boys, was widely believed to be a witch. Persons at their extremity with fever and illness may make unexpected accusations which require the self-confessed victim's nearest kin to take action in order to respect his wishes and restore his health. The survivors may be less obligated to press an accusation, however, after the victim's death. The witches who were believed to have tormented Sunkaru, Konya, and three of Moussa's close relatives were forgotten when these men died.

In seven of the ten sorcery incidents recorded in my notes, motives based upon prior altercations in social relations were admitted by, or attributed to, the sorcerer. These seven included an attack by a bereaved elder (Waliba) against an old enemy (Culoni) who was also thought to be a witch. In five of the seven incidents, men attacked, or were believed to have attacked, their competitors for particular women. In one incident, an elder (Wassa, Case 20) purported to have gotten rid of some undesirable affines. In the three sorcery incidents in which no prior quarrels occurred, the sorcerer acted, or was believed to have acted, in response to suspected witchcraft.

Six of the ten sorcery incidents involved physical misfortune as the stimulus for engaging in sorcery, as the presumed consequence of admitted sorcery, or as the evidence that sorcery had probably occurred. Four of these six incidents involving misfortune were also linked with existing quarrels.

Four of the ten incidents were not triggered by or directly associated with misfortune. In three of these four, men attacked, or were believed to have attacked, their sexual competitors. In the fourth incident which concerned a man who unsuccessfully sought to ensorcell another man in his compound because of suspected witchcraft, neither conflict nor misfortune seems to have preceded the attempt.

Although all of the sorcerers in these ten instances were male, female sorcerers are said to occur, and there were several fragmentary incidents reported where women were in fact involved. Because most of my informants were men, some of the quiet but lively scheming between women may have been missed. I was warned, for example, on several occasions by one woman in my compound to be suspicious of food sent by another woman of the same compound because a marabout had told the informant that the other woman was determined to "poison" me so that I would think about nothing but her, day and night, throughout my stay in the village. This led to some food throwing (in the interest of my well-being) between the two women, which required a discussion by elders before it eventually cooled off.

Sorcery, as opposed to witchcraft, is more directly a consequence of conflicts in interpersonal affairs, but is even less clearly related than witchcraft to the resolution of these conflicts. In only one of the ten sorcery incidents does it appear that "insupportable relationships" were "blasted away." The cases involving Waliba, Kufé, Wali, and Kosita, and a sequence of accusations from the village of Sare Oura suggest that witchcraft, and not sorcery, provides the justification for domestic fission.[21] Sorcery, being primarily a deliberate attempt to manipulate one's relationships with other people, provides a less powerful charter for breaking up the compound than does witchcraft which, because it is more unpredictable and arbitrary, is more dangerous.

It does not seem possible, in the case of lovers' quarrels, to predict which, if either, of the two alternatives will surface. Tamba, for example, was worried about reprisals for the wrong

[21] This does not mean that all cases of residential dispersion involve witchcraft.

he had done to several men whose wives he had married, but he blamed his troubles on the witchcraft of his headman, Culoni, with whom he had no quarrel. Paiti the seer declared that the man whose wife he stole attacked him as a witch and not as a sorcerer. In the episode between Kokudo and Kosita, however, Kosita had taken Kokudo's legally married wife, Kokudo was known to be a witch, and Kosita suspected Kokudo of trying to harm him by sorcery.

Although ten cases is a small sample, sorcery, as opposed to witchcraft, explanations may be more intimately associated with conflicts and less intimately associated with misfortune. This latter possibility would accord with the Badyaranké premise that most suffering is caused by witches. There seemed no way to determine from the evidence of the misfortune alone which explanation would emerge.

Because some three-fourths of the suspicions and accusations of witchcraft did not involve demonstrable, preexisting conflicts, I am reluctant to assume, as most writers on the subject have, that mystical, blame-pinning explanations for misfortune provide an open window to areas of structural disaccord. Occasionally they do, but often they do not.[22] Keith Basso's interpretive and thoughtful analysis of *Western Apache Witchcraft* reflects this conflict-oriented bias which, in light of the Badyaranké data and of reservations expressed by Ames, Douglas, and Turner, should be regarded as questionable and incomplete:

. . . we will make three basic assumptions. . . . The first is that witchcraft accusations may be interpreted as expressions of aggression which stem primarily from interpersonal conflict. . . . The second is that persons involved in accusations — the alleged witch and his accuser — participate in social relationships which tend to foster this conflict. . . . The third assumption is that these relationships have antecedents in the structure of society and, unless that structure is altered, they will recur again and again.[23]

[22] Even Marwick, for example, writes: "This brings to mind the thirty per cent of cases in which no quarrel preceded the believed attack or accusation. In these instances the blame for a misfortune was laid at the door of someone who was not necessarily in a tense relationship with the victim or the accuser. . . . People had to look around for someone to blame" (1965a:291).
[23] Basso 1969:55.

The patterns of suspicion and accusation among the Badyaranké follow no clear mechanical rules; at most, it may be said that witchcraft and sorcery occur between people who live together, and the closer they live, the more likely they are to occur (see Table 3). The frequencies referred to in Figure 3 and Tables 3–6 include several cases not mentioned in the text. The term *accuser* is used to refer to anyone who accused another of witchcraft, openly or secretly, or who urged that a divination be performed or a marabout consulted.

The distributions of witches, accusers, and victims according to approximate age and sex are not particularly revealing. Male witches outnumber female (Table 4), despite the general belief among men that witchcraft is a female attribute. Witches and accusers tend to be adults (Figure 3), whereas victims are more randomly distributed over the age-scale, with peaks at infancy and young adulthood. These peaks are due to the biological fact that mortality among infants is high, and the sociological fact that death among young adults is disruptive. Children below circumcision age are spared the blame for witchcraft death, in spite of the belief that one is born with eyes of the night. The Badyaranké have no explanation why a youthful witch does not kill, other than such remarks as "he is too small." We may induce, however, that to be a witch requires the minimum social and sexual personality conferred at circumcision.

Despite the familiar tensions between co-wives, the undesirability and infrequency of divorce as a solution to relieving such tensions, and the general belief expressed by Badyaranké men that witchcraft attacks are common between co-wives, only one solid instance of such a believed attack was discovered (Table 5). The virtual absence of witchcraft accusations between co-wives means that — in addition to questioning the extent to which witchcraft accusations may be assumed *a priori* to be "indices" of structural conflicts — one might also question the more fundamental assumption that witchcraft accusations are born in hard feeling at all.

Although I cannot convincingly assert that witches and sorcerers or their accusers act as disguised and unwitting tension indices or

152

FIGURE 3 FREQUENCY OF WITCH, ACCUSER, AND
VICTIM ACCORDING TO APPROXIMATE AGE

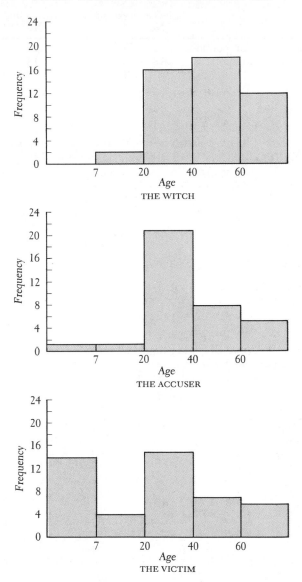

THE WITCH

THE ACCUSER

THE VICTIM

TABLE 3  FREQUENCY OF WITCH-AND-VICTIM AND
ACCUSER-AND-WITCH COMBINATIONS ACCORDING TO COMPOUND

|  | Witch-and-Victim | | Accuser-and-Witch | |
|---|---|---|---|---|
|  | No. | % | No. | % |
| From the Same Compound | 30 | 70 | 23 | 62 |
| From Different Compounds | 13 | 30 | 14 | 38 |
| Total | 43 | 100 | 37 | 100 |


TABLE 4  DISTRIBUTIONS OF WITCH, ACCUSER, AND
VICTIM ACCORDING TO APPROXIMATE AGE AND SEX

|  | Witch | | Accuser | | Victim | |
|---|---|---|---|---|---|---|
| Age | Male | Female | Male | Female | Male | Female |
| 0–7 | 0 | 0 | 1 | 0 | 9 | 5 |
| 8–20 | 2 | 0 | 1 | 0 | 3 | 1 |
| 21–40 | 11 | 5 | 20 | 1 | 10 | 5 |
| 40–60 | 12 | 6 | 5 | 3 | 2 | 5 |
| Over 60 | 5 | 7 | 5 | 0 | 6 | 0 |
| Total | 30 | 18 | 32 | 4 | 30 | 16 |


TABLE 5  ABSOLUTE FREQUENCIES OF WITCH-AND-VICTIM,
ACCUSER-AND-WITCH, AND ACCUSER-AND-VICTIM
COMBINATIONS ACCORDING TO KINSHIP CATEGORIES

| Relationship | Witch-and-Victim | Accuser-and-Witch | Accuser-and-Victim |
|---|---|---|---|
| Mother-Child | 5 | 1 | 3 |
| Full Siblings (dyasé or nmpiaré) | 2 | 1 | 4 |
| Mother's Brother-Sister's son (mbani-nimé) | 4 | 3 | 0 |
| Father-Child | 11 | 5 | 9 |
| Husband-Wife | 2 | 1 | 6 |
| Siblings (fadi) | 2 | 6 | 2 |
| Co-Wives | 0 | 1 | 0 |
| Miscellaneous Affinal | 7 | 9 | 0 |
| Total | 33 | 27 | 24 |

TABLE 6   ABSOLUTE FREQUENCIES OF WITCH-AND-VICTIM,
ACCUSER-AND-WITCH, AND ACCUSER-AND-VICTIM
COMBINATIONS ACCORDING TO MATRILINEAL RELATIONSHIP

|  | Witch-and-Victim | | Accuser-and-Witch | | Accuser-and-Victim | |
|---|---|---|---|---|---|---|
|  | No. | % | No. | % | No. | % |
| Matrilineally Related | 13 | 25.5 | 5 | 10.9 | 7 | 15.2 |
| Non-matrilineally Related | 22 | 43.1 | 22 | 47.8 | 17 | 37.0 |
| Unrelated | 16 | 31.4 | 17 | 36.9 | 6 | 13.0 |
| Same Person | 0 | 0 | 2 | 4.3 | 16 | 34.8 |
| Total | 51 | 100 | 46 | 99.9 | 46 | 100 |

repairmen of the social order, or that they are the offspring of conflict, the few contexts in which misfortune occurred and accusations were not made, and non-blame-pinning solutions were invoked, suggest such explanations may de-fuse suffering when persons fear trouble or wish to avoid it. The illnesses and the deaths of children and of socially unimportant adults are occasionally explained without recourse to blame (Cases 4, 13, 14, 15, 19), and even a socially unsettling death (Case 17) may be explained away if the desire to continue existing relationships is sufficiently strong.

The Badyaranké system of supernatural explanations contributes to social cohesion to the limited extent that the dominant belief, that individual suffering is caused by witches, can be used to advantage — and to the extent that the system offers alternatives through which the dominant belief can be occasionally ignored. Among the Badyaranké, as among the Central African Lele: "Witchcraft is not merely a brutal midwife delivering new forms to society, though it may be this; it is also an aggravator of all hostilities and fears, an obstacle to peaceful co-operation." [24]

[24] Douglas 1963:141.

## CHAPTER SEVEN

# Concluding
# Observations

Each of the structural units of Badyaranké society — the compound, the matrisib, and the village — engages in public rites that provide for the health and well-being of their members. Despite conscientious ritual attention to Kodan, the genies, and ancestors by most of the people, some individuals suffer more than others, and some enjoy more than their share of life's rewards. To explain these exceptional cases, which are always more apparent and more immediate, the Badyaranké refer to an array of beings and forces that interfere with the order that men wish for in their affairs. These beings and forces provide explanations which may be arranged along a continuum, with witchcraft at one end (a blame-pinning theory of misfortune), through the various sorcery techniques, contracts with forest sprites, exchanges with genies, forgotten contracts with shrines, inadvertent possession by genies, and with direct acts of God and the violations of numerous taboos at the other end. To the Badyaranké, acts of God and the taboos are asocial theories of suffering which explain misfortune in terms that do not require another person to be blamed.

## THE WITCH'S ROLE

The Badyaranké believe that most human misfortune is caused by witches who seem like ordinary people, with whom one carries on day-to-day affairs, but who participate in an invisible conspiracy against their friends and neighbors. Unfortunate events which occur despite regular precautions may be dealt with as if they were due to human agency; the sanctions by which men have learned to control one another are externalized in an effort to achieve mastery over events such as death and physical decline, which a stoic would consider to be beyond human control. The human veneer of the witch's being is held responsible, as a hostage, for the arbitrary suffering which his other being brings to men. Belief in witchcraft allows the accused person to be treated as a monster to whom the norms and proprieties of village life do not apply. In some cases the belief that a relative or friend is also a hideous creature from beyond the edge of vision provides socially useful advantages, for it enables individuals to sever once intimate relationships that have become strained and undesirable. It may not be easy to denounce one's brother, for example, but it can be if he is also someone else. The timely occurrence of misfortune generally provides the justification, as well as the incentive, for such dramatic breaches.

While envy, hatred, and the imminence of severed social ties sometimes act as cues for determining who the witch (or the accuser) might be, friendship, love, and the desirability of continued ties may sometimes influence who the witch may not be. But the real horror of witchcraft, as the Badyaranké see it, lies in the fact that the witch might be anyone, even one's most cherished neighbor, if he has compelling obligations to other witches to repay souls. In the accusations known to me, most of the witches were not involved in diffuse and irreconcilable quarrels, nor were they previously hated by their victims or by their accusers. Witchcraft is above all a theory of misfortune, and people suffer, whether or not they are enmeshed in social situations from which they would like to exit but for some reason cannot.

## SEERS, GENIES, AND SHRINES

Seers are similar in all respects to witches, except that instead of direct and wanton murder, they are said to exchange the lives of their dependents for the bounty that the sprite is able to provide. Prosperity acquired through farming, hunting, or fishing suggests to the Badyaranké that a person has engaged in secretive contracts with forest sprites and, thus, that he is a seer. Suspected seers are not physically punished for their privileged commerce as witches sometimes are, but they are brought to the public eye and condemned through gossip by their indignant and less prosperous neighbors. Although contracts with sprites provide a potential theory of misfortune, such beliefs become identified with individuals who are enjoying the other side of the coin from misfortune, whose prosperity thereby becomes construed as a vague threat to other people's well-being.

Wealth, talent, and renown may also be acquired from genies, but courting them is extremely dangerous. Individuals who succeed through the genies' favor or at the genies' expense risk being visited by madness, hysteria, sickness, and death. A person, such as the hunter Nokoli, who displays exceptional skill and who then incurs sickness or an accident would be judged by others to be a seer and to have brought the hardship upon himself.

At the lower end of the blame-pinning continuum, individuals who cause themselves or others to suffer misfortune because of forgotten contracts with shrines or accidental contact with polluting creatures are not blamed, criticized, or punished for their actions. Such transgressions are often admitted by the persons involved, and suggest no mystical or vindictive profiteering. Witchcraft and the pollution taboos, at opposite ends of the blame-pinning scale, are the two explanations most frequently associated with misfortunes. Given that the Badyaranké hold one another responsible for individual suffering, the many taboos that are believed to influence infant mortality seem to provide respite for people who are trying to live and work together.

E. H. Winter in his discussion of Amba witchcraft distinguished between existential ideas that define the way the world is, and normative ideas that define, given the world, how one should behave in it. Beliefs about witches comprise one segment of ideas concerning the nature of reality. The Badyaranké, like the Amba, "believe that the sun rises in the east every morning and sets in the west every evening, . . . and that there are witches who kill and eat their fellow men." [1] Thus, the question "Why witches?" equates with asking "Why the sun?" or "Why trees?" People know about the sun and trees, however, because they see them. But witches and other spirits reveal themselves in the visible and tangible world through the unfolding of events, and their recognition as being behind these events follows processes more akin to intuitive or aesthetic judgment than to empirical diagnosis.

Reaction to any particular accident, sickness, or death may be influenced by many variables: victim's age, his social and financial status, the reputation of the marabout consulted, and the survivors' (if any) good or bad rapport with their neighbors. One would know, for example, by examining the deceased, if a particular death was due to snake bite. But one would need to know the mourners in order to predict whether the snake was someone (a witch), or whether sorcery, genies, sprites, or something else had caused the snake to bite. Mystical explanations are not inherent in the symptoms of the misfortune, and thus there is little self-evident connection between a particular type of misfortune and a particular supernatural agency. Events are connected to explanations through the often arbitrary occurrence of witchcraft accusations, or through the mediation of social circumstances which sometimes favor alternatives whereby no one is held responsible. [2]

[1] Winter 1963:285–286.
[2] Robin Horton has argued that the social circumstances surrounding a misfortune help the diviner in selecting the supernatural agent. An argument between lineage members, for example, might suggest that an illness was sent by

The witch, who hides in an invisible dimension and who only reveals himself through what could be described as indirect or circumstantial evidence, is nevertheless conceived according to a model with some basis in experience. The Badyaranké word *umadisé*, which I have glossed as *seer*, is consistently associated with indeterminate states of being. The two most powerfully polluting creatures, the nightjar and the dwarf antelope, are said to have the "eyes of the night," and are habitués of the twilight, that shadowy period that belongs to neither day nor night. I never thought to ask if tortoises, caterpillars, eggs, or pigeons are umadisé, but all are considered to be dangerous by the Badyaranké. It may be speculated that they are ambiguous with respect to important criteria of Badyaranké classification. For example, tortoises live both on land and in the water, are quadrupeds with scales and without teeth, and lay eggs; caterpillars and eggs are born, but not yet born. The pigeon is used in folklore to refer to an outsider in the family; the Badyaranké proverb "Pigeon be content with chaff" is recited to an uninvited guest who eats with the family but has no right to complain about the food. Thus, a pigeon fits this marginal role because it lives in the forest and eats "in the family," i.e., where the women winnow.

Deformed children who presumably mix parts from the human and spirit worlds, newly circumcised boys who are no longer posé but not yet wambani (men), and unburied corpses which are no longer with the living but not yet with the dead — all are considered to be powerful seers. Individuals whose behavior is considered unusual because they exceed normal expectancies are assimilated against their will into the class of beings which are umadisé. Others who fall short of the norms for success were observed to admit being umadisé to gain importance. Thus the

---

ancestors who are concerned with such matters. Choice of explanation among the Badyaranké depends less on the final authority of a diviner; a marabout suggests answers, but they are not necessarily accepted. Although witchcraft is the most ready explanation, it is sometimes avoided, even if diagnosed by a diviner, if the persons involved wish to avert disruption. In such cases, rather than an explanation being determined by the prior social circumstances, the explanation is chosen on the basis of its influence on subsequent relations.

upper and lower limits of social performance intercept in the world of the night, that threshold between the everyday world and the world of the spirits. The ambiguities of beings such as the nightjar, antelope, initiate, deformed child, and pigeon are elaborated to the fullest possible extent in the Badyaranké conception of the witch, in whom all order is juxtaposed and confused.

Against destruction that might be caused by witches, the Badyaranké have created a number of counterforces, the most important — or at least the most dramatic — of which is the masked dancer (concurra) who enters the village once each year, or when there is an emergency, to locate, humiliate, and sometimes beat witches. The mask by itself is considered powerless and the wearer by himself may be a non-seer, but once he puts on the mask, he acquires the ability to shriek in a strange language, has eyes to see the world of the night, and has the unimpeded right to punish witches. His judgment is said to be infallible and his powers are unrestricted, even by the village chief.

The witch's human appearance masks the monster within. In order to recognize and defeat witches, the Badyaranké have created an equivalent, but opposed, power by putting a frightening mask over an ordinary human. Through the masked dancer they open a twilight between the human and spirit worlds which is the dimension seen only through eyes of the night. In this twilight, the masked dancer pursues the witch; his purpose is to purify the community by identifying and humiliating those who are thought to be involved in witchcraft. During the hours that the masked dancer roams through the village, the rules by which men normally govern themselves are temporarily suspended.

# Bibliography

Ames, David
1959 "Belief in 'Witches' among the Rural Wolof of the Gambia."
*Africa* 29(3):263–273.
Appia, Beatrice
1944 "Note sur le génie des eaux en Guineé." *Journal de la Société des Africanistes* 14:33–41.
Bailey, F. G.
1964 "Capital, Saving and Credit in Highland Orissa (India)." In Raymond Firth and B. S. Yamey (Eds.), *Capital, Saving and Credit in Peasant Societies.* Chicago: Aldine Publishing Company, pp. 104–132.
Basso, Keith H.
1969 *Western Apache Witchcraft.* Anthropological Papers of the University of Arizona, No. 15. Tucson: The University of Arizona Press.
Beidelman, T. O.
1963 "Witchcraft in Ukaguru." In John Middleton and E. H. Winter (Eds.), *Witchcraft and Sorcery in East Africa.* New York: Frederick A. Praeger, pp. 57–98.
Bohannan, Laura
1958 "Political Aspects of Tiv Social Organization." In John Middleton and David Tait (Eds.), *Tribes without Rulers: Studies in African Segmentary Systems.* London: Routledge and Kegan Paul Ltd., pp. 33–66.
———, and Paul Bohannan
1953 *The Tiv of Central Nigeria.* London: International African Institute.
Bohannan, Paul
1957 *Justice and Judgement among the Tiv.* New York: Oxford University Press for the International African Institute.

163

1958 "Extra-Processual Events in Tiv Political Institutions." *American Anthropologist* 60:1–12.

Carreira, Antonio
1963 "Alguns aspectos da influência da lingua Mandinga na Pajadinca." *Boletim Cultural da Guiné Portuguesa* 18(71):345–383.

Colson, Elizabeth
1966 "The Alien Diviner and Local Politics among the Tonga of Zambia." In Marc J. Swartz, Victor W. Turner, and Arthur Tuden (Eds.), *Political Anthropology*. Chicago: Aldine Publishing Company, pp. 221–228.

Douglas, Mary
1963 "Techniques of Sorcery Control in Central Africa." In John Middleton and E. H. Winter (Eds.), *Witchcraft and Sorcery in East Africa*. New York: Frederick A. Praeger, pp. 123–142.
1966 *Purity and Danger: An Analysis of Concepts of Pollution and Taboo*. New York: Frederick A. Praeger.
1967 "Witch Beliefs in Central Africa." *Africa* 37(1):72–80.

Ducos, G. E.
1964 "Parallèle Badiaranké-Peul, limité à deux points de structure." *Journal of African Languages* 3:75–79.

Evans-Pritchard, E. E.
1937 *Witchcraft, Oracles and Magic among the Azande*. Oxford: Clarendon Press.

Forde, Daryll
1964 *Yakö Studies*. London: Oxford University Press for the International African Institute, pp. 210–233.

Fortes, M., and G. Dieterlen (Eds.)
1965 *African Systems of Thought*. London: Oxford University Press for the International African Institute.

Foster, George M.
1960–61 "Interpersonal Relations in a Peasant Society." *Human Organization* 19(4):174–178.
1965 "Peasant Society and the Image of Limited Good." *American Anthropologist* 67:293–315.

Gessain, Monique
1958 "Note sur les Badyaranké (Guinée, Guinée Portugaise et Sénégal)." *Journal de la Société des Africanistes* 28:43–89.

Gluckman, Max
1963 *Custom and Conflict in Africa*. Oxford: Basil Blackwell.

Greenberg, Joseph H.
1963 *The Languages of Africa*. Bloomington: Indiana University Press.

Horton, Robin
1967 "African Traditional Thought and Western Science." *Africa* 37(2):155–187.

Hulstaert, Rev. Pere G.
1965 "La Sorcellerie chez les Mongo." In M. Fortes and G. Dieterlen (Eds.), *African Systems of Thought*. London: Oxford University Press for the International African Institute, pp. 165–170.

Huntingford, G. W. B.
1963 "Nandi Witchcraft." In John Middleton and E. H. Winter (Eds.), *Witchcraft and Sorcery in East Africa*. New York: Frederick A. Praeger, pp. 175–186.

Kluckhohn, Clyde
1962 *Navaho Witchcraft*. Boston: Beacon Press.
Krige, E. J., and J. D. Krige
1943 *The Realm of a Rain-Queen*. London: Oxford University Press for the International Institute of African Languages and Cultures.
Krige, J. D.
1947 "The Social Function of Witchcraft." *Theoria*. 1:8–21.
Kuper, Hilda
1965 *An African Aristocracy: Rank among the Swazi*. London: Oxford University Press for the International African Institute.
Labouret, Henri
1934 *Les Manding et leur langue*. Paris: Librairie Larose.
Lestrange, Monique de
1950 "Génies de l'eau et de la brousse en Guinée française." *Études guinéennes* 4:3–24.
Levy-Bruhl, Lucien
1963 *Le Surnaturel et la nature dans la mentalité primitive*. Paris: Presses Universitaires de France.
Lowie, Robert H.
1920 *Primitive Society*. New York: Boni and Liveright.
Mair, Lucy
1969 *Witchcraft*. New York: World University Library.
Malinowski, Bronislaw
1926 *Crime and Custom in Savage Society*. London: Kegan Paul, Trench, Trubner and Co.
Marwick, M. G.
1952 "The Social Context of Ceŵa Witch Beliefs." *Africa* 22(3):215–233.
1965a *Sorcery in Its Social Setting: A Study of the Northern Rhodesian Ceŵa*. Manchester: Manchester University Press.
1965b "Some Problems in the Sociology of Sorcery and Witchcraft." In M. Fortes and G. Dieterlen (Eds.), *African Systems of Thought*. London: Oxford University Press for the International African Institute, pp. 171–191.
Maybury-Lewis, David
1967 *Akwẽ-Shavante Society*. Oxford: Clarendon Press.
Middleton, John
1963 "Witchcraft and Sorcery in Lugbara." In John Middleton and E. H. Winter (Eds.), *Witchcraft and Sorcery in East Africa*. New York: Frederick A. Praeger, pp. 257–276.
————, and E. H. Winter (Eds.)
1963 *Witchcraft and Sorcery in East Africa*. New York: Frederick A. Praeger.
Mitchell, J. Clyde
1952 "A Note on the African Conception of Causality." *The Nyasaland Journal* 5(2):51–58.
1956 *The Yao Village: A Study in the Social Structure of a Nyasaland Tribe*. Manchester: Manchester University Press.
Monteil, Vincent
1964 *L'Islam noir*. Paris: Éditions du Seuil.
Murdock, George Peter
1960 *Social Structure*. New York: The Macmillan Company.

Nadel, S. F.
1952 "Witchcraft in Four African Societies: An Essay in Comparison."
*American Anthropologist* 54:18–29.
Schapera, I.
1952 "Sorcery and Witchcraft in Bechuanaland." *African Affairs.* 51:41–52.
Simmons, William S.
1967a "Social Organization among the Badyaranké of Tonghia, Sénégal."
*Bulletins et Memoires de la Société d'Anthropologie de Paris.*
*Cahiers du Centre de Recherches Anthropologiques* 7:59–95.
1967b "The Supernatural World of the Badyaranké of Tonghia (Sénégal)."
*Journal de la Société des Africanistes* 37:41–72.
Swanson, Guy E.
1964 *The Birth of the Gods: The Origin of Primitive Beliefs.* Ann Arbor:
The University of Michigan Press.
Turner, Victor W.
1957 *Schism and Continuity in an African Society: A Study of Ndembu
Village Life.* Manchester: Manchester University Press.
1964 "Witchcraft and Sorcery: Taxonomy Versus Dynamics." *Africa*
34(4):314–325.
Whiting, Beatrice Blyth
'1950 *Paiute Sorcery.* Viking Fund Publications in Anthropology, No. 15.
New York: The Viking Fund.
Wilson, Monica
1951 *Good Company: A Study of Nyakyusa Age-Villages.* London: Oxford
University Press for the International African Institute.
Wilson, W. A. A.
1959 "Linguistic Tour of Portuguese Guinea." *Boletim Cultural da Guiné
Portuguesa* 14(56):569–601.
1961 "Numeration in the Languages of Guinea." *Africa* 31:372–377.
1965 "A Reconstruction of the Pajade Mutation System." *Journal of
West African Languages* 2(1):15–20.
Winter, E. H.
1963 "The Enemy Within: Amba Witchcraft and Sociological Theory."
In John Middleton and E. H. Winter (Eds.), *Witchcraft and Sor-
cery in East Africa.* New York: Frederick A. Praeger, pp. 277–299.

# Index

Fula Kunda tribe, 14, 39, 41, 42, 47, 48, 49, 63, 64, 74, 81, 82, 90, 93, 117, 119, 122, 127, 130, 131, 133, 134
Fulani, 11, 14 (see also Fula Kunda tribe and Peul Fouta tribe)

Gambia, 47, 84, 137
genies (dyinné), 35, 51–53, 60, 72, 75, 76, 84–89, 93, 94, 111, 113, 135, 136, 147, 156, 158, 159
Gessain, Monique, 3, 11 (see also Monique de Lestrange)
Gessain, Robert, 3
Gluckman, Max, 99, 145
God (Kodan), 19, 35, 51, 53–55, 65, 70–72, 74, 77, 110, 147, 156, 157
goats, 13, 21, 23, 24, 42, 46, 52, 119, 141
Greenberg, Joseph H., 12
Guinea, Republic of, 6, 9, 11, 12, 40, 47, 48, 63, 80, 84, 87, 88, 102, 103, 112, 132, 135, 140–142

harmattan, 9, 12
headmanship, 33–35, 36, 38, 72
Horton, Robin, 159–160
housing, 1, 5, 28, 29

inheritance, 20–24
Islam, 3, 5, 8, 13, 40, 49, 51, 54, 55, 71, 93, 121

joking relationship, 15, 17, 81, 141

kinship terms, 19–26
Kluckhohn, Clyde, 108, 111, 112, 140, 144, 145
kola nuts, 20, 23, 24, 26, 34, 46, 54, 82, 94, 128

Labouret, Henri, 17
Lele tribe, 155
Lestrange, Monique de, 71 (see also Monique Gessain)
Levy-Bruhl, Lucien, 145
Lowie, Robert H., 14
Lugbara tribe, 108, 109

Mair, Lucy, 109, 145
Malinowski, Bronislaw, 144
Manding tribe, 8, 11, 13, 14, 17, 51, 53–55, 64, 74, 122

marabout, 3, 35, 42, 51–54, 60–62, 65, 85, 89, 96, 101, 102, 115, 117, 119, 120, 122, 124, 125, 127–131, 133–136, 142, 147–150; amulets made by, 55–62
marketing, of peanuts, 35, 40, 81
marriage, 17, 20–26, 28, 31, 32, 39
Marwick, M. G., 28, 144, 145, 148, 151
masked dancer, 78, 161
matrisib, 6, 14–26, 32, 33, 40, 99, 156; sacrifice by, 65–67
Middleton, John, 108, 144
Mitchell, J. Clyde, 145
monkeys, 50, 142
Murdock, George P., 14
music, 1, 40, 41, 79

Navaho tribe, 108, 111, 112, 140
Ndembu tribe, 28
nightjar, 65, 67, 68, 119, 131, 160, 161 (see also pollution taboos)
ninkinanka (giant serpent), 71, 72
Nyakyusa tribe, 93

omens, 10, 97, 122, 126, 127, 129, 141
owl, as transformed witch, 2, 3, 10, 53, 97, 109, 126, 127

palm wine, 2, 6, 13, 24, 34, 41, 49, 54, 89, 130
patronym, 6, 17, 18, 40
Peul Fouta tribe, 13, 39, 42, 43, 47, 48, 49, 74, 118, 122
pollution taboos, 51, 67, 68, 69, 70, 73, 82, 96, 111, 119, 120, 128, 129, 147, 156, 157, 158, 160
Portuguese Guinea, 11, 13, 16, 47, 102, 133
possession, 87, 88, 156
postpartum sex taboo, 51, 70, 128, 135

sada, 35, 53, 55, 60, 61, 65, 122, 128
sheep, 13, 21, 23, 24, 42
shrines, 51, 62, 63, 66, 72, 104, 141, 146, 156, 158; caterpillar shrine, 65, 68; for barren women, 64; nightjar shrine, 65, 68, 131
Simmons, William S., 12
sorcery, 42, 51, 58, 61, 104, 111, 121, 125, 134, 141, 142, 152, 156, 159;

sorcery (*Cont.*)
  contrasted with witchcraft, 146,
  149–151
soul, 3, 19, 54, 71, 74, 75, 80, 95,
  97, 98, 101, 121, 122, 126, 129–
  131, 134, 137–139, 143, 147, 157
spells, 62, 125
sprites (*foncoté* and *ufann*), 4, 75,
  76, 84, 87, 89–94, 108, 111, 147,
  156, 159
Swanson, Guy E., 144

Tambacounda, 4, 22, 115, 134
Tanzania, 93
taxes, 20, 24, 26, 45
Tenda language group, 12
Tiv tribe, 93, 101
Tonghia: description, 5–6, 13, 14, 40,
  41; history, 14, 40, 45, 51, 52, 113;
  location, 2
totems, matrisib, 14–18

Turner, Victor W., 28, 109, 145,
  146, 151

*ufann* (*see* sprites)
Uganda, 108

Velingara, 14, 47, 139

wage labor, 20–22, 47, 48, 136, 137
Whiting, Beatrice Blyth, 144
widow inheritance, 15, 24, 32, 136
Wilson, Monica, 93
Wilson, W. A. A., 12
Winter, E. H., 108, 109, 159
witches: feast, 96, 97; Fula Kunda,
  97, 98; as inverted beings, 108–109
Wolof tribe, 22, 42, 47, 74, 146
work groups (*palau* and *patumbare*),
  35, 45, 46

Yakö tribe, 111
yearly cycle, 12–13, 39, 46